France

France

BY LIZ SONNEBORN

Enchantment of the World™
Second Series

Children's Press®

An Imprint of Scholastic Inc.

NEW YORK TORONTO LONDON AUCKLAND SYDNEY
MEXICO CITY NEW DELHI HONG KONG
DANBURY, CONNECTICUT

Frontispiece: Old building in Provence

Consultant: Brett Bowles, Associate Professor of French Studies, Indiana University, Bloomington

Please note: All statistics are as up-to-date as possible at the time of publication.

Book production by The Design Lab

Library of Congress Cataloging-in-Publication Data

Sonneborn, Liz.
  France / by Liz Sonneborn.
     pages cm. — (Enchantment of the world. Second series)
  Includes bibliographical references and index.
  ISBN 978-0-531-25600-8 (lib. bdg. : alkaline paper)
  1. France—Juvenile literature. I. Title.

DC17.S664 2013
944—dc23   2012047113

1 2 3 4 5 6 7 8 9 10 R 22 21 20 19 18 17 16 15 14 13

France

Contents

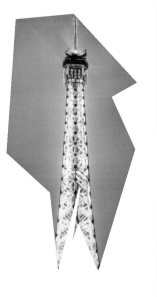

Cover photo:
Eiffel Tower

Northern coast

Gallic rooster

CHAPTER ONE

The Heroine of France

I N ABOUT 1425, IN THE TOWN OF DOMRÉMY IN northeastern France, a thirteen-year-old peasant girl named Joan of Arc began hearing voices. At the time, France was fighting a war with England, a conflict that began long before Joan was even born.

Joan was convinced that the voices were those of the Catholic saints Michael, Catherine, and Margaret. Being a devout Catholic, Joan wanted to obey their commands, but she could not see how that would be possible. The voices insisted that she lead the French army in expelling the English invaders from France.

Opposite: **The Entrance of Joan of Arc into Orléans, by Jean-Jacques Scherrer**

Battling the English

Unsure what to do, Joan tried for years to ignore the voices she was hearing. But by the time she was sixteen, they had become so loud and insistent that she felt she had no choice

The Heroine of France **9**

FRANCE

- ● Cities of over 200,000 people
- ○ Other cities
- ✪ National capital

0   150 miles

0   150 kilometers

NETHERLANDS

North Sea

UNITED KINGDOM

Calais   Dunkerque

BELGIUM

Lille

English Channel

Valenciennes

Dieppe

Cherbourg   Le Havre   Rouen   Amiens   Sedan

LUXEMBOURG

Saint-Malo   Bayeux   Caen   Giverny   Reims   Verdun

GERMANY

Brest   Seine R.   Paris   Châlons-en-Champagne   Metz   Nancy   Strasbourg

Rennes   Chartres   Vaucouleurs

Lorient   Carnac   Le Mans   Orléans   Troyes   Mulhouse

AUSTRIA

Angers   Tours   Auxerre

Saint-Nazaire   Nantes   LIECHTENSTEIN

Bourges   Dijon   Besançon

La Roche-sur-Yon   Niort   Poitiers   Loire R.   SWITZERLAND

ATLANTIC OCEAN

La Rochelle   Moulins   Taizé   Lake Geneva

Limoges   Clermont-Ferrand   Vichy   Lyon

Tulle   Saint-Étienne   Chambéry

Bay of Biscay

Bordeaux   Lascaux caves   Valence   Grenoble   Vanoise Natl. Park

ITALY

Garonne R.   Rhône R.   Écrins Natl. Park   Mercantour Natl. Park

Mende   Rodez   Avignon

Mont-de-Marsan   Cévennes Natl. Park

Bayonne   Pau   Toulouse   Nîmes   Aix-en-Provence   Nice

Pyrénées Occidentales Natl. Park   Montpellier   Apt   MONACO

Canal du Midi   Marseille   Cannes

SPAIN   Perpignan   Gulf of Lion   Toulon

Bastia

Calvi

Corsica   Aléria

Cerbère   Ajaccio

ANDORRA   Mediterranean Sea   Bonifacio

France

but to act. She traveled to the town of Vaucouleurs and told the French troops there that she wanted to help them fight and defeat the English. Baffled by the strange girl, they sent her home. Months later, she was back and more determined than ever. Joan was so passionate about her mission that she was finally given soldiers to command.

Joan rode with the troops onto the battlefield, inspiring them as they stormed into the city of Orléans, which was then occupied by the English. Joan's army won the fight and drove the English away.

King Charles VII of France agreed to allow Joan of Arc to travel with the army to Orléans.

The conflict between France and England, now called the Hundred Years' War, continued. Joan also kept on fighting, until May 1430, when she was captured by a group of Frenchmen who supported the English cause. They sold her to the English, who put her in prison.

For months, Joan was interrogated. She was accused of holding beliefs that were against the official doctrines of the Catholic Church. She was also accused of not observing "proper" women's behavior. Joan refused to admit to anything. Instead, she stated that she could communicate directly with God. In a daring escape attempt, she even jumped from her tower cell. Finally, isolated and injured, she signed a confession and was given a life

sentence. But shortly thereafter she took back her confession and was sentenced to death. Joan was tied to a wooden stake and set on fire. She was only around nineteen years old when she died on May 30, 1431.

Joan of Arc was gone, but her story lived on in many remarkable ways. For several centuries, she was merely a historical figure in accounts of the Hundred Years' War. But,

Joan of Arc was executed in the city of Rouen, in northern France.

beginning in the early nineteenth century, she emerged as a celebrated heroine who inspired some of the world's greatest composers, painters, novelists, and playwrights. In 1920, she was named a saint by the Catholic Church. More recently, Joan has become something of a pop culture icon, depicted in everything from movies and television shows to video games and comic books.

A Symbol of France

Through the years, Joan of Arc emerged as something more than just a great French heroine. She became a symbol of France itself. Every May 1, the French acknowledge her birthday with a celebration. The festivities were especially elaborate in 2012, which marked the six hundredth anniversary of the year it is believed she was born. The city of Orléans commemorated that birthday with a two-week-long festival enjoyed by more than forty thousand people. The signature event was a re-creation of her triumphant march into Orléans.

While the French agree that Joan of Arc is a national symbol, they have not always been of one mind over what that symbol means. Over the years, many different factions of the French people have claimed Joan as their own. For instance, since the 1980s, the National Front, a far-right French political party, has featured Joan's image on much of their literature and even erected a statue of her outside its Paris headquarters. The party largely blames France's ills on new immigrants. It likens these immigrants to the invading English Joan wanted to expel from France.

On the six hundredth anniversary of Joan of Arc's birth, the city of Orléans held a grand celebration in her honor.

During France's 2012 presidential election, the sitting president Nicolas Sarkozy challenged the National Front's view of Joan. Hoping to score his own political points, he visited Domrémy-la-Pucelle and gave a lofty speech in which he tried to associate his candidacy with Joan of Arc. In the end, though, neither Sarkozy nor Marine Le Pen, the National Front candidate, gained much from their efforts to use Joan for their own ends. Another candidate, François Hollande, won the election.

Joan of Arc remains close to the heart of the French people. As Sarkozy said, "The place of Joan of Arc was not in gilded legend, but in the history of France. . . . Joan is the incarnation of the most beautiful French virtues." Those virtues might be up for debate, but they include a passion for justice and freedom, a willingness to embrace noble ideals, and an ability to face difficulty with dignity and resolve. But perhaps the most French thing about Joan of Arc was her devotion to France itself. Today, there are many divisions among the French people along the lines of class and religion. But nearly all share a tremendous love of France and a ferocious pride in being French.

François Hollande of the Socialist Party became president of France in 2012.

C H A P T E R

T W O

A Diverse Land

16

THROUGHOUT ITS HISTORY, FRANCE HAS BEEN blessed by its geography. It has served as a crossroads of Europe, linking itself and the continent to the world beyond. Its many rivers provided an easy means of traveling to neighboring countries in Europe, while the Atlantic Ocean and Mediterranean Sea provided access to places farther away in North America, South America, and Africa. In the interior, rich soil and a pleasant, temperate climate created ideal conditions for farming, providing a comfortable environment and plenty of food for a growing population.

Opposite: **Green fields brighten the French countryside.**

Borders and Boundaries

France is the largest country in western Europe and the forty-third largest country in the world. France shares borders with eight other countries. To the southwest are Spain and Andorra. To the northeast are Belgium and Luxembourg. And to the east are Germany, Switzerland, Italy, and Monaco.

France's Geographic Features

Area (metropolitan France): 212,935 square miles (551,500 sq km)

Highest Elevation: Mont Blanc, 15,771 feet (4,807 m) above sea level

Lowest Elevation: Rhône River delta, 7 feet (2 m) below sea level

Longest River: Loire River, 634 miles (1,020 km)

Largest Lake: Lake Bourget, 17 square miles (44 sq km)

Hottest Month: July, average high temperature in Paris of 75°F (24°C)

Coldest Month: January, average low temperature in Paris of 34°F (1°C)

Longest Border: With Spain, 387 miles (623 km)

Shortest Border: With Monaco, 2.7 miles (4.4 km)

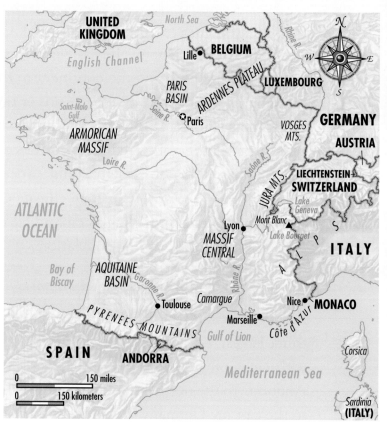

Most of France's land borders follow natural boundaries created by mountains. The two principal mountain ranges are the Pyrenees, located along France's border with Spain, and the Alps, which run along most of its border with Switzerland and Italy. France's tallest peaks are found in the Alps. Its highest mountain is Mont Blanc, which rises to 15,771 feet (4,807 meters).

France also borders four bodies of water. The Atlantic Ocean lies to the west, and the Mediterranean Sea lies to the southeast. The North Sea and the English Channel abut France to the northwest. Known to the French as La Manche, the English Channel separates France from its northern neighbor, the United Kingdom. Since 1994, a train line called the Eurostar has run through a tunnel under the channel, linking the two nations.

Pink rocks line the coast of northwestern France.

The Rhône River flows through many French cities, including Arles, Avignon, and Lyon (above).

Part of the southern border between France and Germany follows the Rhine River. The Rhine is one of several major river systems that water France. The most important is the Seine, which begins in eastern France and flows northwest, through Paris, before emptying into the English Channel at the port of Le Havre. The Rhône, the deepest river in France, runs north to south and links the city of Lyon to the Mediterranean Sea. The Loire has the distinction of being the longest river in France. It flows across the center of the country and into the Bay of Biscay, a gulf of the Atlantic.

The Cities of France

When most people think about city life in France, they immediately picture Paris, the capital and largest city. But the country has many other vibrant cities.

The Greeks founded Marseille, the oldest city in France, in about 600 BCE. It is located on the coast of the Mediterranean Sea near the mouth of the Rhône River. Today, it is the second-largest city in France and a bustling port. The sunny city features beautiful beaches and large outdoor markets. Immigrants, particularly from northern and western Africa, have long been drawn to Marseille. As a result, it has the most diverse population of all French cities.

Lyon (below), France's third-largest city, is known for its sophistication. Located on the Rhône and Saône Rivers, it was founded by the Romans in 43 BCE. Lyon has long been a leading producer of silk and textiles, and is now a center for banking and industry. The city

is renowned for its architecture, ranging from ancient Roman arenas to grand churches to narrow passageways called *traboules*, which run through buildings connecting one street to the next. It is also home to many museums, galleries, theaters, and high-end shops. To food lovers, though, it is beloved for its many excellent restaurants, particularly its *bouchons*—small family-owned bistros that offer delicious traditional French food at modest prices.

Toulouse (above) in southern France, is nicknamed La Ville Rose (Pink City) because of the rose-colored brick used in many of its buildings. Located on the east bank of the Garonne River, the city is famed for its historical monuments and churches. It is also the center of France's aeronautic and high-tech industries. The University of Toulouse, founded in the thirteenth century, trains many of France's top scientists and engineers.

In the Mediterranean Sea, about 100 miles (161 kilometers) from the French mainland is the island of Corsica. Except for brief periods of British and German occupation, Corsica has been under the control of the French government since 1796. The mainland and Corsica are often referred to as metropolitan France. The area includes a total of 212,935 square miles (551,500 square kilometers) of land.

At various times in its history, France has claimed territory in other parts of the world. It now holds lands in North America, South America, the Caribbean Sea, the Pacific Ocean, the Indian Ocean, and Antarctica. Five overseas possessions are official departments of France, which means they have representatives within the national government. Four of these departments are islands: Mayotte and Réunion in the Indian Ocean, and Guadeloupe and Martinique in the Caribbean Sea. The fifth and largest overseas department is

Terre Adélie

In 1837, French explorer Jules Dumont d'Urville headed an expedition into the western Pacific Ocean in search of uncharted territory he could claim for France. During the voyage, Dumont d'Urville discovered a portion of the continent of Antarctica. It was an extremely cold and forbidding area, but Dumont d'Urville called it Terre Adélie (Adélie Land) as a tribute to his wife, Adèle. Today, the area is home to a large population of penguins and the staff of the Dumont d'Urville Station, a French research base.

French Guiana, which is located on the northern coast of South America between Brazil and Suriname.

Other French possessions, officially designated as overseas territories, include French Polynesia, New Caledonia, Saint-Barthélemy, Saint Martin, Saint-Pierre and Miquelon, and Wallis and Futuna. Altogether, France's overseas territories are home to more than two million people.

Corsica was formed by volcanic eruptions. It is the most mountainous island in the Mediterranean Sea.

Landscapes

Scattered the world over, France's overseas territories feature a wide array of terrains, from the dense rain forests of French Guiana, to the mountains of New Caledonia, to the frozen lands of the French Antarctic territories. But even within the borders of metropolitan France, there is an exceptionally broad range of landscapes.

In the north and west, France is mostly covered with flat plains and gentle hills. Because of the fertile soil of these lowlands, this area has the largest concentration of farms. Moving south, the land becomes more elevated. South-central France features a great plateau called the Massif Central, which includes about one-sixth of the total area of the country. To the far southeast and southwest are mountainous areas dominated by the towering Pyrenees and Alps mountain ranges. Small mountains are found in the Jura range, to the north of the Alps, and in the Vosges range in the northeastern portion of the country.

Drizzly days are common in western France.

Climate

France also has a wide variety of climates. Western France, along the Atlantic coast, has the highest rainfall of any place in metropolitan France. Because of westerly winds blowing in from the ocean, the area experiences frequent light rain showers throughout the year. Sunny skies give way to rain clouds with little notice. This region also has fairly cool summers and mild winters. Farther inland, summers are hotter and winters are colder, but the area receives less precipitation than the coastal region. The coldest places in France are in the mountainous regions. The peaks of the Alps, for instance, are covered in snow year-round.

Although much of France has a comfortable, temperate climate, the Mediterranean coast is particularly known for its pleasant weather. In southeastern France and on the island of Corsica, winters are warm and summers are dry and hot. In the warmer months in particular, vacationers from throughout Europe and beyond flock to southern France to enjoy its pristine beaches and cloudless skies.

People flock to the French coast during the warm summer months.

Deadly Heat

In 2003, Europe experienced its hottest summer on record. France was hit worst of all. In July and August, the French suffered through seven days of temperatures of at least 104 degrees Fahrenheit (40 degrees Celsius). Most of France usually experiences mild summers. Even on hot days, the air temperature cools down at night. But during this heat wave, night temperatures stayed high. Most French homes are not air-conditioned, so they remained stifling at all hours. An investigation by the French National Institute of Health found that 14,802 people in France died because of the heat. Most were elderly, and some of them had been left alone. Because August is traditionally vacation time in France, many of these victims' family members and much of the staff at public health institutions were away when this heat wave occurred. The crisis prompted sharp criticism of the government and caused the nation to reexamine its care for the elderly.

The Natural World

WITH ITS MILD CLIMATE AND FERTILE, WELL-WATERED soil, much of France provides an excellent environment for many types of plant life. Today, farms cover almost half of France. About another one-third of the country is forested.

Opposite: **Towering fir trees cover many slopes in the French Alps.**

Forests, Farms, and Flowers

Until the early twentieth century, France's once vast forests were shrinking as large numbers of trees were harvested for timber and fuel. But the French government was able to reverse the trend through an aggressive replanting program. Now more than 130 different types of trees grow in France, a larger number than in any other European country.

Forests of oak and beech trees cover much of north-central France. Chestnut trees are common in the high plateaus of the Massif Central, while tall pines flourish in the hilly south. Eucalyptus trees imported from Australia dot the Provence region of the southeast.

The Trees of the Canal du Midi

A lush urban forest of forty-two thousand plane trees forms a canopy over the Canal du Midi, a channel dug in the seventeenth century that connects the city of Toulouse to the Mediterranean Sea. In 2006, scientists discovered that many of these two-hundred-year-old trees were diseased. Although the sick trees have to be cut down, the government hopes to plant enough young, healthy trees to preserve the beauty of this popular historic site.

Near the Mediterranean, the warm climate is perfect for olive and fruit trees. Much of the Mediterranean coastal lands and the island of Corsica are also covered with dense evergreen shrubs called maquis. These plants have a unique place in French history. The French Resistance movement, which opposed the German occupation of France during World War II, named itself the Maquis after this hearty vegetation.

Many food crops are grown on French farms. The soil is particularly good for growing grains, such as wheat and barley. French farms also produce a wide array of fruits and vegetables. Some farms grow flowers, which are both sold as blossoms and used in the perfume industry. Flowers frequently grown in France include roses, carnations, tulips, and irises. The Provence region is famed for its lavender fields. Each spring, tourists flock to the region to see the bright purple lavender plants and breathe in their wonderful scent.

In cities, many French enjoy visiting formal gardens. Among the most popular are the Jardin des Plantes, a vast botanical garden with a school for students studying plants, and the Tuileries Garden, a gathering spot for Parisians that dates back to the sixteenth century. The French Ministry of Culture promotes France's traditional love of gardening by compiling an official list of *jardins remarquables*, or "remarkable gardens."

Rows of lavender paint the landscape purple in Provence.

The National Flower

The iris holds the honor of being the national flower of France. Its beautiful purple blooms have long been associated with the country. Beginning in the twelfth century, the kings of France decorated their flags, robes, and palaces with a stylized image of the iris that is now called a fleur-de-lis.

The Gardens of Giverny

In 1883, French painter Claude Monet moved to the small town of Giverny. He had long loved how the natural foliage of the Seine River valley was dappled by the warm summer light. At his home there, he designed a beautiful garden that included all the plants and colorful flowers he longed to paint. Now considered a pioneer of modern art, Monet created many of his greatest later masterpieces while painting outdoors in Giverny. In the 1970s, Monet's house and garden were fully restored, and they are now open to the public. More than half a million people visit the grounds each year to see the real landscapes that inspired this great painter.

Animal Life

France provides a welcoming environment for a variety of animals. Lowland areas in the countryside are home to many different mammals, including wild boars, wolves, foxes, otters, and badgers. France's deer population has doubled in the past several decades, and roe and red deer are common.

The mountainous regions provide comfortable habitats for brown bears, marmots, and alpine hares. Less common creatures, such as the ibex and the chamois, also live in the mountains. The ibex, a wild goat with giant, curving horns, is found in the Alps. The chamois, a type of antelope, has black stripes under both eyes on its white face. Chamois have been seen high up on Mont Blanc, the tallest mountain peak in France.

Many small mammals, such as squirrels, rabbits, and mice, are equally at home in the country and the city. Birds, such as

thrushes and owls, are also common in urban centers. Eagles and falcons soar above mountainous areas, while migratory birds from Africa spend the winter in southern France. These birds include herons, egrets, and brightly colored flamingos. Aquatic animals, such as dolphins, lobsters, and crayfish, live off the French coast, and France's rivers teem with perch, carp, pike, and trout.

Both male and female ibexes have horns. The male's horns can reach 55 inches (140 cm) long.

The Gallic Rooster

For centuries, the Gallic rooster has been a symbol of France. During the French Revolution, an image of the rooster adorned flags carried by the rebels. It has since appeared on French coins, stamps, and the official seal of the French Republic. Today, a rooster decorates the gates of the Elysée Palace, the residence of the French president, and the players of France's national soccer team proudly wear jerseys with a rooster logo.

Preserving Nature

In recent years, the French government has worked hard to preserve areas of natural beauty and to protect endangered habitats of both animal and plant life. There are now ten national parks in metropolitan France and its overseas possessions. The largest is the Guiana Amazonian Park in French Guiana, which includes more than 13,000 square miles (33,600 sq km) of tropical rain forest. In addition, France has designated more than three hundred areas as nature reserves.

Camargue horses are strong, rugged, and intelligent.

Zarafa the Giraffe

In October 1826, an unlikely ambassador arrived in the French port city of Marseille—a giraffe named Zarafa. The animal was a gift from Muhammad Ali, Viceroy of Egypt, to French king Charles X.

In the spring, Zarafa—from the Arabic word for "charming"—made the trek from Marseille to Paris on foot. She attracted massive crowds wherever she went. As the first giraffe in France, Zarafa quickly became a sensation. When she reached the capital, more than one hundred thousand Parisians came out to greet her. Her image soon appeared on all sorts of items, from fabric to wallpaper to porcelain dishes. Fashionable women even began using wire frames to create sky-high hairstyles that mimicked Zarafa's long neck.

Zarafa made her home in the Jardin des Plantes, the largest botanical garden in France, until her death in 1845. Even today, she continues to fascinate the French. In 2012, she was the subject of a new animated film for children and an exhibition at the Jardin des Plantes.

One of the most popular reserves is in the Camargue, a region in southern France along the Mediterranean Sea. The Camargue reserve extends over part of the flat, wet Rhône River delta. The area serves as a nesting ground for many birds, including flamingos.

The Camargue also supports herds of wild horses. These small, white horses live in the region's wetlands, their only natural habitat.

Creating the Nation

Human beings have lived in what is now France for tens of thousands of years. Early people in the region were hunters and gatherers. Perhaps the most spectacular artifacts of these prehistoric peoples are paintings found in the Lascaux caves near the village of Montignac. In about 18,000 BCE, artists painted extraordinary images of bulls, horses, bison, wolves, and rhinoceroses on the cave walls. Carnac, in southwestern France, also contains evidence of early humans. In that small town, prehistoric people arranged about three thousand heavy boulders so that they look like a forest of stones. Why they created this formation, known as the Carnac stones, is still a mystery.

Opposite: **Prehistoric people painted almost two thousand images in the Lascaux caves.**

Celts and Romans

Between about 2000 and 100 BCE, tribal peoples called the Celts settled in much of northwestern Europe. They migrated from the east to what is now France by about 450 BCE. The Celts were rural people, who lived mostly by hunting, fishing, and raising livestock.

In 58 BCE, Julius Caesar led an army of Roman troops into France, which the Romans called Gaul. At the time, the Romans ruled a vast empire, with territories in Europe, Asia, and northern Africa. The Celts, who had been united by the great warrior Vercingetorix, fought the invaders, but they were defeated in 51 BCE.

For the next four hundred years, Gaul was part of the Roman Empire. Officials in Rome forced the Gauls to pay taxes and serve in the Roman army. But Roman rule also benefited Gaul. During this period, the Romans built towns and roads in Gaul and developed trade in the region. In addition, the Romans introduced the Gauls to the concepts of a standard code of laws and a central government with power over a large territory. Both ideas would be important in the development of France as a nation.

The influence of the Romans is still visible in France. The nation is home to some of the best-preserved Roman ruins

The Romans built the Pont du Gard in the first century CE.

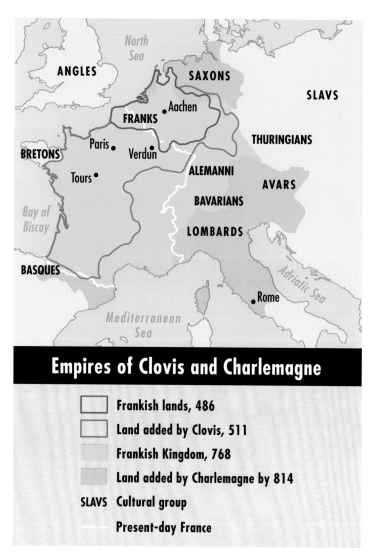

Empires of Clovis and Charlemagne

- Frankish lands, 486
- Land added by Clovis, 511
- Frankish Kingdom, 768
- Land added by Charlemagne by 814
- **SLAVS** Cultural group
- — Present-day France

anywhere in the world. The city of Nîmes in southern France boasts the Maison-Carrée, a two-thousand-year-old Roman temple, and the Pont du Gard, a massive aqueduct bridge the Romans built to carry water into the city.

Early France

By the fifth century CE, the Roman Empire was in decline. At this time the Franks, a Germanic tribe, recognized a good opportunity for themselves. They crossed the Rhine and took control of Gaul. The Franks' association with Gaul gave the region a new name—France.

From 481 to 511, Clovis, the leader of the Franks, ruled the first great kingdom in France. He adopted the Christian religion, which soon spread among the people of his realm. The greatest Frankish king, however, was Charlemagne, whose reign lasted from 768 to 814. The territory he brought under his rule included not just what is now France, but also Germany and parts of Italy and Spain. Charlemagne called his realm the Holy Roman Empire.

Hard Times

During the following centuries, French society was organized by an economic system called feudalism. Under this system, kings granted land and special privileges to people of high social status called nobles. In exchange, nobles pledged loyalty to the monarch and offered aid in military missions. These included the Crusades, a series of wars fought by European Christians to wrest control of the holy city of Jerusalem, in what is now Israel, from Muslims (people who practice the religion of Islam). The vast majority of French people were neither kings nor nobles, but peasants. They made a meager living by working the lands controlled by nobles.

In the 1300s, Europe was struck by the bubonic plague, a deadly disease often called the Black Death. In France, nearly one-third of the population died. During that same period,

The Bayeux Tapestry

The Bayeux Tapestry (detail, left) is an extraordinary piece of embroidered cloth, which measures 231 feet (70 m) long. It is more than a beautiful work of art. It is also an important historical document. Likely created during the twelfth century, its embroidered scenes depict the history of the Norman Conquest of 1066, during which William, the duke of Normandy, seized the English crown. The incredible details of the thread work have provided historians with a wealth of information about the period—from the types of armor soldiers used to the kinds of buildings they constructed to the way both French and English men cut their hair. Today, the tapestry is in the Bayeux Tapestry Museum in the city of Bayeux, in northwestern France.

France became embroiled in a series of conflicts with England called the Hundred Years' War (1337–1453). The war finally ended in a victory for France.

The growth of the Protestant religion in France led to battles between Catholics and French Protestants, called Huguenots. The St. Bartholomew's Day Massacre of 1572, the bloodiest event of these conflicts, resulted in the murder of thousands of Huguenots at the hands of Catholics.

The St. Bartholomew's Day Massacre began in Paris and spread to other cities.

The Bourbon Dynasty

Henry IV was the first of a line of kings in France called the Bourbon dynasty. He was a Huguenot, but he converted to Catholicism when he took the throne in 1589. To end the religious violence, he issued the Edict of Nantes in 1598. The edict stated that Catholicism was the official religion of France, but it said that French Protestants had a legal right to practice their religion.

The greatest Bourbon monarch was Louis XIV, who ruled for nearly seventy-two years (1643–1715). Known as the Sun King, he believed that monarchs should have absolute power and that they were placed on the throne by the will of God. The Palace of Versailles, just outside Paris, was a symbol of his authority and strength and served as the base from which he ruled. The king spared no expense in constructing and decorating Versailles. His support of the arts inspired a flowering of French painting, architecture, and drama.

During his reign, Louis XIV also waged a series of wars, which extended his rule into what are now Belgium, Luxembourg, and the Netherlands. France emerged as the leading power in Europe. It also had an empire with extensive claims in North America and Asia. By the time of his death, the Sun King ruled over an enormously powerful nation.

The Revolution

Louis XIV's successors had far less vision and political skill than he had. Louis XV sponsored several expensive, unsuccessful wars, which left the kingdom near bankruptcy. Forced

Versailles

In the suburbs of Paris lies perhaps the most famous home in the world. The Palace of Versailles was built for King Louis XIV (right) in the seventeenth century as a display of his power and wealth. Other French kings continued construction of Versailles until the French Revolution. Today, the palace and its gardens are a popular tourist attraction.

The palace has many grand rooms and halls. The most famous is the Hall of Mirrors (below), which is decorated with more than three hundred mirrors. In the seventeenth century, mirrors were luxury items that only the very rich could afford. The gardens at Versailles are filled with elaborate fountains, pools, and statues.

Other buildings on the palace grounds include the Grand Trianon and the Petit Trianon. Constructed from elegant pink marble, the Grand Trianon was a house Louis XIV built to have privacy from the French court. In the eighteenth century, Louis XV built a smaller, less elaborate structure, the Petit Trianon. His son Louis XVI later gave it to his young wife, Marie Antoinette, as a gift. Nearby, she entertained her friends at a replica of a country farm village. Tired of the luxuries of the court, they enjoyed pretending they were poor peasants, although they were in fact living on one of the most extravagant estates ever built.

to raise taxes, he became extremely unpopular among the French. His grandson Louis XVI similarly angered his subjects by spending huge sums to support the American Revolution, during which colonists in what is now the United States fought for their independence from British rule. The French people also resented the extravagance of the Versailles court during a period in which many peasants were starving. Among educated French people, the ideas of philosophers such as Voltaire and Jean-Jacques Rousseau inspired them to question the absolute power of monarchs and to challenge the special privileges granted to nobles and the Catholic clergy.

Voltaire

One of France's most inventive writers and thinkers, Voltaire popularized many of the ideas about justice and equality that inspired the French Revolution. Born François-Marie Arouet in 1694, he found success at a young age by writing clever plays and poems under the name Voltaire. Many of his works, which also included novels and essays, criticized social inequity in France, where nobles and clergymen had so much and peasants had so little. Voltaire's writings upset the nobles, who called for his arrest. He also angered many Catholic officials by arguing in favor of religious freedom and calling for the end of the persecution of Protestants in France.

After many years living abroad, Voltaire settled on an estate in Ferney in east-central France in 1760. There, he treated the peasants living on his land with respect and generosity. Voltaire died in Paris in 1778, eleven years before the French Revolution. The people of Ferney honored Voltaire by renaming the town Ferney-Voltaire.

By 1789, it was clear that Louis XVI had lost the support of the French. They demanded that the king convene the Estates-General to deal with the financial crisis. The Estates-General was a legislative body made up of representatives of the three major estates, or social classes, in French society: the clergy (the First Estate); the nobles (the Second Estate); and everyone else, including rural peasants, urban laborers, and more prosperous professionals and merchants (the Third Estate). For the Third Estate representatives, the meeting was

Tensions ran high at a meeting of the Estates-General in 1789.

frustrating. The clergy and the nobles voted together to block the reforms the Third Estate believed were needed to create a more just society. In response, the Third Estate representatives abandoned the Estates-General and set up their own governing body for France, the National Assembly, in order to fairly represent the will of the people as a whole.

The situation grew increasingly tense. The king began to gather troops near Paris. Fearing that the king was planning to turn his troops on his own people, an angry mob stormed the Bastille prison, a symbol of the hated regime, on July 14, 1789. Throughout France, hungry peasants began to riot. The French Revolution had begun.

A crowd attacked the Bastille prison in order to free prisoners and capture the guns and gunpowder stored there.

Marie Antoinette opposed reforms in France. She became a symbol of the royal family's lack of concern for the average person.

The National Assembly wrote a document called the Declaration of the Rights of Man and of the Citizen. It stated that all men were "born equal in rights" and held that the people, not the king, should govern France. It echoed the revolutionaries' motto *Liberté, Egalité, Fraternité* (Liberty, Equality, Fraternity).

As the National Assembly took the reins of government, it ended the feudal system, abolished the privileges of the nobles, and seized land from the Catholic Church. Louis XVI and his family at first cooperated with the National Assembly's plan to create a constitutional monarchy. In this kind of government, the monarch is the head of state but is limited in power by a constitution. However, in July 1791 the royal family fled Paris for Austria, Marie Antoinette's home country. The family was caught near the border. With their credibility ruined, the king and queen were imprisoned, convicted of treason against France, and eventually executed in 1793.

These developments allowed a group of radical revolutionaries known as the Jacobins to take power over more moderate groups. Aristocrats and anyone suspected of being enemies of the revolution were sentenced to death during what became known as the Reign of Terror. Many were killed with a guillotine, a device that dropped a blade to slice off a person's head. During the Reign of Terror, tens of thousands of people were murdered. At the same time, the Jacobins declared war against the other monarchies of Europe in an attempt to spread revolution.

Thousands of people, including the king, were executed by guillotine during the French Revolution.

The Rise of Napoléon

During the chaos following the Reign of Terror, a gifted general named Napoléon Bonaparte led France to a series of victories over foreign enemies. After seizing control of the French government in 1799, he restored peace and stability to France. He used his popularity to declare himself emperor five years later. Although Napoléon had the power of a king, he ruled France largely by the ideals embraced during the revolution. He oversaw the creation of France's first comprehensive set of laws, the Civil Code, which remains the basis for France's legal system today.

After carrying out reforms at home and restoring France to prosperity, Napoléon set out to conquer Europe by military force. By 1812, he had much of the continent under his control. But he overplayed his hand by invading Russia, where bitter winter weather and disease nearly destroyed the French army. Two years later, Russia joined with other European powers to defeat Napoléon. In 1815, Napoléon tried to reclaim his empire. After a few months, he lost his final battle to an army of British and Dutch troops at Waterloo in present-day Belgium.

Napoléon's Empire, 1812

- French Empire
- States dependent on Napoléon
- States allied with Napoléon
- States against Napoléon

Napoléon (seated on white horse) gained control of much of Europe in the early nineteenth century.

A World Leader

After Napoléon's defeat, the Bourbon dynasty of kings briefly retook the French throne, but their rule was unpopular. In 1830, the last of the Bourbon line, Louis Philippe, took power as a constitutional monarch. Nicknamed the Citizen King, he had supported reform during the revolution, even though the executed king Louis XVI was his second cousin. In 1848, however, an ailing economy and the denial of voting rights to a growing population of urban workers sent protesters into the streets. The king tried to send troops in to end the protests, but his own soldiers rejected his rule. Louis Philippe gave up his crown and lived the rest of his life in England.

After the revolt of 1848, France held its first election in which all male citizens could vote. The voters chose Louis Napoléon, the nephew of Napoléon Bonaparte, as their new president. In

In the 1800s, Paris became a city of wide boulevards and grand buildings.

1852, he took complete control of the government and declared himself emperor. Ruling as Napoléon III, he oversaw the reconstruction of Paris into a vibrant, modern capital. He also raised France's international profile, by establishing new overseas colonies and entering into competition with Great Britain.

Napoléon III's military adventures led to his downfall. After his army was defeated in 1871 during the Franco-Prussian War, the humiliated emperor left France. The country again became a republic, with elected leaders. Struggling after the disastrous conflict with Prussia (now part of Germany), France slowly rebounded.

As its economy improved and its empire grew, France became a world leader in the fields of science and technology. Louis Pasteur was a pioneer in the field of microbiology, the study of life-forms that are so small they can be seen only through a microscope. He made many breakthroughs in preventing disease, including developing vaccines for diseases such as rabies and inventing a process that stopped germs from growing in milk. This became known as pasteurization. In 1903, physicist and chemist Marie Curie became the first woman to win the Nobel Prize, for her research on radioactivity. During this period, France also emerged as the world's

Émile Zola

Émile Zola was one of France's greatest novelists and humanitarians. He was born in Paris on April 2, 1840. After years of struggling as a writer, he gained fame for a series of novels that portrayed the lives of ordinary French people realistically. His masterpiece *Germinal* (1885) explores the relationships of different classes of people during a coal-mining strike.

In 1895, Zola was outraged when a captain in the French army, Alfred Dreyfus, was convicted of treason. Like many other French intellectuals, Zola believed Dreyfus was innocent. He thought Dreyfus had been found guilty, not because he had done anything wrong, but because he was Jewish. At the time, prejudice against Jews was common in France. In a newspaper, Zola published an angry letter to the president of France titled *"J'accuse"* ("I Accuse"). In it, he accused the French army of framing Dreyfus and the government of covering it up. The letter drew attention to the case and eventually Dreyfus was freed. Zola, however, was convicted of libel (publishing a false and damaging statement) and had to flee France to avoid going to jail. He later returned to Paris, where he died in 1902. Zola is still considered a hero in France for his willingness to confront power and corruption in the quest for justice.

foremost center of art and literature. Claude Monet, Paul Cézanne, Paul Gauguin, and many more painters brought their own unique perspectives to art. Meanwhile, writers such as Émile Zola, Gustave Flaubert, Charles Baudelaire, and Arthur Rimbaud influenced literature around the world.

The World Wars

Two enormous wars in the early twentieth century were fought, in part, on French soil. World War I (1914–1918) pitted France, the United Kingdom, Russia, the United States, and other allies

French soldiers prepare to attack during World War I.

against Germany, Austria-Hungary, and the Ottoman Empire. Over the course of four years, much of the bloodiest fighting occurred on the Western Front, which included northeastern France. France and its allies eventually won the war, but that victory came at an extremely high price. During the war, 4.2 million French soldiers were wounded and 1.4 million were killed, including one-quarter of all French men between the ages of eighteen and twenty-seven.

During the 1930s, France suffered through the world-wide economic downturn called the Great Depression. The period also saw the rise of the Nazi Party in Germany. Fearing the Nazi leader Adolf Hitler would draw France into another war, the French allowed him to take part of

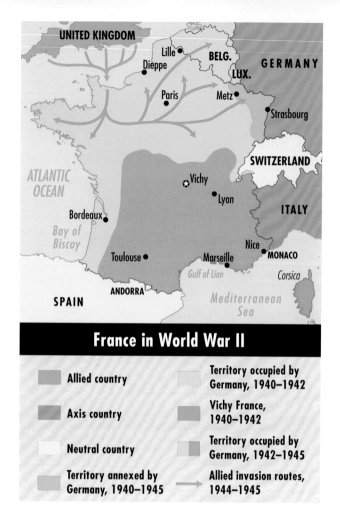

France in World War II

- Allied country
- Axis country
- Neutral country
- Territory annexed by Germany, 1940–1945
- Territory occupied by Germany, 1940–1942
- Vichy France, 1940–1942
- Territory occupied by Germany, 1942–1945
- Allied invasion routes, 1944–1945

Czechoslovakia, a country bordering Germany. This did not ensure peace, however. When Hitler's army invaded Poland in September 1939, France and the United Kingdom declared war on Germany. During World War II (1939–1945), these countries would be joined by the United States, the Soviet Union (a large country consisting of Russia and other parts of eastern Europe and western Asia), and other nations to form the Allied forces.

In May 1940, Germany invaded France. The next month, Paris fell. Members of the French government fled south to the resort town of Vichy. They agreed to cooperate with Germany and signed a cease-fire. At first, Germany occupied northern France, while the Vichy government, under the thumb of Germany, ruled southern France. By 1942, however, as the Allies started to turn the tide of the war against the Nazis, all of France was occupied.

Some French people refused to accept the Vichy government and wanted to continue fighting Germany. In France, the French Resistance, also known as the Maquis, waged a guerrilla war against the Germans. They eventually merged with the Free French movement led from London, England, by French general Charles de Gaulle. In June 1944, Allied forces landed on the beaches of Normandy in northern France. Two months later, they freed Paris from the Germans. De Gaulle became the president of the provisional government of France.

A Modern Nation

After the war ended in 1945, France worked to recover and rebuild. Using economic aid from the United States, France repaired buildings damaged by the war, improved its transportation systems, and modernized its factories. To

About two hundred thousand French people were active in the resistance movement.

General and President

Charles de Gaulle was one of the country's important political leaders in the postwar era. He was born November 22, 1890, into a distinguished family in the city of Lille in northern France. De Gaulle entered the military and served in the French army in World War I, becoming a prisoner of war in Germany. After the war, he resumed his military career and wrote several books about strategy.

During World War II, de Gaulle strongly opposed France's surrender to Germany. He became the commander in chief of the Free French forces based in London and fought to liberate France. When the Allies drove the Germans from France, de Gaulle headed up a provisional government. He soon resigned from the presidency to protest a new French constitution because he felt it gave too much power to the National Assembly, the principal legislative body.

De Gaulle returned to politics in 1958, when, with the nation deeply divided over the Algerian War, the French president asked the old war hero to serve as prime minister. France soon adopted a new constitution. As de Gaulle had wanted, this constitution granted the president extensive power.

De Gaulle became president in January 1959. In this position, de Gaulle worked to grant independence to Algeria. He also tried to make France the dominant force in Europe. In the wake of massive protests by students and workers fighting for education reform, de Gaulle resigned from the presidency in 1969. He died of a heart attack on November 9, 1970.

further promote economic growth by increasing trade with its European neighbors, France joined West Germany, Italy, Belgium, Luxembourg, and the Netherlands to form the European Economic Community (EEC)—also known as the Common Market—in 1957.

In 1945, France granted new political rights and economic opportunities to the residents of certain colonies. However, revolts against French rule erupted in several other colonies. In 1954, after nearly a decade of attempting to suppress the independence movement, France was forced to give up its claims to Indochina (now Vietnam, Laos, and Cambodia). Shortly afterward, another colonial war began in the North African colony of Algeria. Disputes over how to deal with the revolution there nearly tore the French government apart. On the brink of civil war, France adopted a new constitution in 1958 and granted most of its other African colonies independence by 1960. With increased constitutional powers, newly elected president Charles

French tanks crash through a barricade in Algeria as Algerians begin their fight for independence.

de Gaulle initiated the withdrawal of France from Algeria as well, which became independent in 1962. Since that time, France has retained strong cultural and economic ties to its former colonies. Large numbers of immigrants have come to France from former colonies in search of a better life. Their cultural diversity changed the ethnic makeup of France, which today has the third-highest proportion of immigrants in the world behind only the United States and Canada.

By 1968, France had completed its postwar recovery and become one of the wealthiest and most modern nations in the world. But students and workers who felt alienated by

Protesting students battle the police in 1968.

President de Gaulle's authoritarian leadership held massive demonstrations demanding reform. Their demands led to sweeping changes in the educational system, including reduced tuition at universities and greater government funding. Other reforms gave regional and local institutions more power to make decisions.

Despite some periods of economic difficulty, over the last thirty years France has remained one of the most powerful and prosperous European nations. It was a founding member of the European Union (EU) in 1993. Building on the older EEC, the European Union is a political, cultural, and economic association of twenty-seven nations spread across the continent. The EU's primary goals are to provide a high standard of living for all residents, promote democracy and peace, and allow Europe to compete economically with North America and Asia. The EU allows free trade among its member states, so goods produced in one country are not taxed when they are shipped to another country. It also supports strong government-sponsored social programs, such as universal health care. Seventeen EU countries, including France, began adopting a common currency, the euro, in 1999.

For many years, the EU and the euro were very successful. But a worldwide economic downturn beginning in 2008 left smaller, less prosperous countries, such as Greece and Spain, virtually bankrupt and wealthier EU countries, such as France and Germany, under pressure to support their neighbors. The ultimate fate of the European Union will shape the political and economic challenges France will face in the years to come.

The Fifth Republic

On September 22, 1792, France became a republic—a form of government in which the people and their elected representatives hold the power. But throughout its history, the country has seen periods of republican rule intermixed with periods when it was under the thumb of kings, emperors, and dictators. As a result, France's current government—called the Fifth Republic—is fairly recent. It began on October 4, 1958, when a new constitution went into effect. Although the constitution has been amended several times since then, it established the basic guidelines by which the French government still functions today.

Opposite: **The National Assembly meets in the Palais Bourbon, in Paris.**

The Executive Branch

The government of France, like that of the United States and Canada, is made up of three branches—the executive, the legislative, and the judicial. The French system combines elements of two systems: presidential democracies like the United States, in which the president is the most powerful figure, and parliamentary democracies like in the United Kingdom, in which the legislature plays the leading role.

In France, executive power is shared between a president and a prime minister. The president is elected by popular vote, with every French person eighteen or older eligible to cast a ballot. The president serves a five-year term and can run for reelection once. He or she is both the head of state and the commander in chief of France's armed forces.

The prime minister is formally appointed by the president but typically represents the majority party in the National Assembly, the larger and more powerful of the French government's two lawmaking bodies. As the head of the government, the prime minister oversees the Council of Ministers, which is similar to the Cabinet in the United States' executive branch. Each minis-

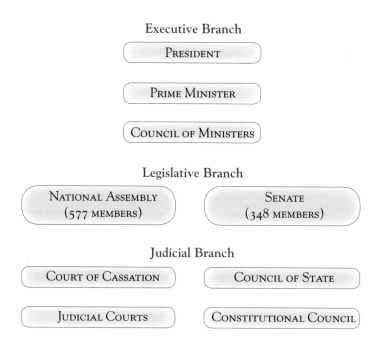

NATIONAL GOVERNMENT OF FRANCE

Executive Branch

PRESIDENT

PRIME MINISTER

COUNCIL OF MINISTERS

Legislative Branch

NATIONAL ASSEMBLY
(577 MEMBERS)

SENATE
(348 MEMBERS)

Judicial Branch

COURT OF CASSATION

COUNCIL OF STATE

JUDICIAL COURTS

CONSTITUTIONAL COUNCIL

Jean-Marc Ayrault became prime minister of France in 2012.

ter heads part of the national government dealing with a specific area. For instance, there are ministers in charge of defense and veterans affairs; higher education and research; public works; sports; culture and communication; and the economy, finance, and industry. Ministers are appointed by the president, acting on the recommendations of the prime minister.

In many countries that have both a president and a prime minister, the president plays a largely ceremonial role while the prime minister actually runs the government. The French constitution of 1958, however, divides power between these positions. The president typically oversees France's dealings with other countries, while the prime minister focuses on domestic policy. According to the constitution, the president is supposed to represent the French people directly and be above political parties. He or she has the authority to dissolve the National Assembly and call new legislative elections.

The City of Light

Perhaps the world's most beautiful city, Paris is both the capital of France and its largest urban center. Located in north-central France about 90 miles (145 km) from the English Channel, Paris and the surrounding area have a population of more than twelve million.

The Seine River flows through its center. Within the river are two islands, the Île de la Cité and Île St.-Louis. Île de la Cité, which was the location of the original city of Paris, is the site of the historic Notre-Dame Cathedral.

Paris has long been a center of intellectual pursuits and education, earning it the nickname the City of Light. It remains a cultural capital, boasting many universities, libraries, and museums. The most renowned museum is the Louvre, which houses the greatest art collection in the world. Paris is also a center for the performing arts, including concerts, ballet, and opera.

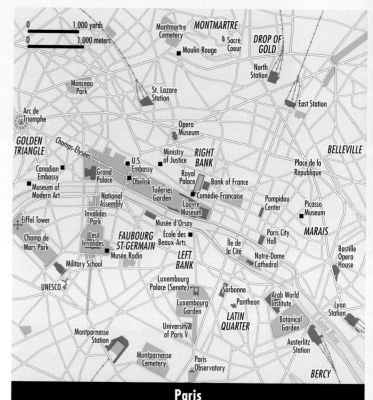

Paris

Among its many theater companies is the Comédie-Française, which has performed classic French plays for more than three hundred years.

Paris is filled with beautiful monuments, including the Eiffel Tower (left) and the Arc de Triomphe. But many tourists are just as impressed by its wide boulevards and amazing shops. They enjoy browsing the offerings at its hundreds of bookshops, perfumeries, art galleries, and clothing boutiques. Restaurants offer a range of mealtime experiences, from gourmet dinners prepared by the world's finest chefs to light snacks at comfortable cafés.

The legislative branch is made up of a parliament, or lawmaking body. France's parliament has two houses—the Senate and the National Assembly.

The Senate consists of 348 members. All but twenty senators are from metropolitan France (mainland France and Corsica) and France's five overseas departments. Eight other senators come from the six overseas territories. The remaining twelve represent French citizens living abroad in other countries.

Senators serve six-year terms. French voters do not elect senators. Instead, they are elected by an electoral college made up of elected officials from the nation's departments, or subdivisions within the country. Every three years, one-third of the Senate seats are up for election.

In the French Senate, the left-wing, or more liberal parties, sit on the left side of the room as viewed from the president's seat. Right-wing parties sit on the right side.

The National Assembly has 577 seats. Of these, 555 are reserved for metropolitan France and 22 for overseas regions and territories. Members of the National Assembly are called deputies. They are elected directly by voters and serve five-year terms. The National Assembly has more responsibility and power than the Senate in proposing and passing new laws. If the two houses disagree on an issue, the National Assembly makes the final decision. The National Assembly can also remove the prime minister from power by majority vote.

French citizens line up to vote in the 2012 presidential election.

French Elections

France usually holds national elections every five years, first for the presidency, and then for the National Assembly. French law places strict limits on how much money each candidate can spend on advertising so that no one has an unfair advantage. On a Sunday in the spring, voters cast their first ballot. If no one gets more than half the votes in the first round of elections, the voters return to the polls the next Sunday to choose between the top two candidates. In elections for the National Assembly, there may be three or four candidates in the second

French people rally in support of François Hollande, the Socialist Party candidate for president in 2012. He won the election.

round, depending on the first-round counts. Whoever gets the largest number of votes in the second round is the winner.

France has many political parties, which sometimes form coalitions to help them win elections. Among the largest parties are the French Socialist Party (PS) and the Union for a Popular Movement (UMP). In recent years, as popular concern over the European Union, immigration, and the economic recession has grown, an extreme right-wing party known as the National Front has gained in popularity.

In May 2012, French citizens went to the polls and, in the second round of voting, elected a new president. French Socialist Party candidate François Hollande beat UMP candidate Nicolas Sarkozy, the sitting president who was running for reelection. The two candidates ran a heated race, which concentrated on their differing views of how best to improve France's struggling economy and manage troubles within the European Union. In June 2012, a coalition led by the PS also won a majority of seats in the National Assembly at the expense of a conservative coalition led by the UMP.

Courts and Laws

The French court system has two branches—judicial courts and administrative courts. Judicial courts hear civil and criminal cases involving individuals. These include some specialized courts, such as juvenile courts that handle cases involving young people and commercial courts for business disputes. People who disagree with the decisions made by judicial courts can challenge them through appeals courts.

"La Marseillaise"

France's "La Marseillaise" is among the most famous national anthems in the world. It was written in 1792, during the French Revolution, by army captain Claude-Joseph Rouget de Lisle while he was stationed in the city of Strasbourg. France had declared war on Austria and Prussia, and the mayor of Strasbourg asked Rouget de Lisle to write a marching song to rally the French soldiers.

His anthem was quickly embraced by the French people. Army volunteers from the city of Marseille sang it as they marched to Paris. Parisians dubbed the patriotic song "La Marseillaise," or "Song of Marseille."

French lyrics	English translation
Allons enfants de la patrie,	Rise up, children of the fatherland
Le jour de gloire est arrivé!	The day of glory is here!
Contre nous de la tyrannie	Against us is tyranny,
L'étendard sanglant est levé!	The bloody flag is raised!
Entendez-vous dans les campagnes,	Can you hear in the countryside
Mugir ces féroces soldats?	The roar of these fierce soldiers?
Ils viennent jusque dans nos bras	They come into our midst
Égorger nos fils, nos compagnes!	To cut the throats of your sons, your companions!
Aux armes, citoyens!	To arms, citizens!
Formez vos bataillons!	Form your battalions!
Marchons! Marchons!	March! March!
Qu'un sang impur	Let their impure blood
Abreuve nos sillons!	Water our fields!

The French Flag

The flag of France consists of three vertical bands: blue on the left, white in the middle, and red on the right. The flag traces its origins to the French Revolution. During that conflict, the hats of Paris militiamen were adorned with cockades—round decorations made of ribbons. The ribbons were blue and red, colors that appeared on the coat of arms of Paris.

In 1789, cockades of blue, white, and red became part of the official uniforms of the National Guard, the new French police force. White had long been associated with France and in the past had been the dominant color on its flags. The next year, a tricolor flag inspired by these cockades became an official symbol of France, and in 1794 it became the official national flag.

The highest appeals court is the Court of Cassation. It can set aside a verdict if it finds a lower court did not interpret the law correctly or did not follow proper procedure.

Administrative courts rule on disputes against government bodies and on challenges to government regulations. The highest body in the administrative court system is the Council of State. It can rule on whether or not decisions made by the French government obey France's laws. This court thus has the power to strike down policies crafted by the executive branch. It also advises the French government about the legality of laws under consideration. The Constitutional Council is made up of nine judges, three each appointed by the president, the Senate, and the National Assembly. It hears challenges to specific laws that may violate the French constitution. The council examines laws only after the National Assembly has passed them, but before the president has signed them.

Unlike the American system, once a law is put into place, it cannot be challenged as unconstitutional.

Regional and Local Governments

Since the 1970s, France has granted increasing power to regional and local governments. Today, France is divided into twenty-seven regions. Twenty-two are in metropolitan France, and five correspond with the overseas departments of French Guiana, Guadeloupe, Martinique, Mayotte, and Réunion. In all, France has ninety-six administrative subdivisions, or departments, which are in turn subdivided into about thirty-seven thousand municipalities, or communes. Each of these divisions has its own elected officials.

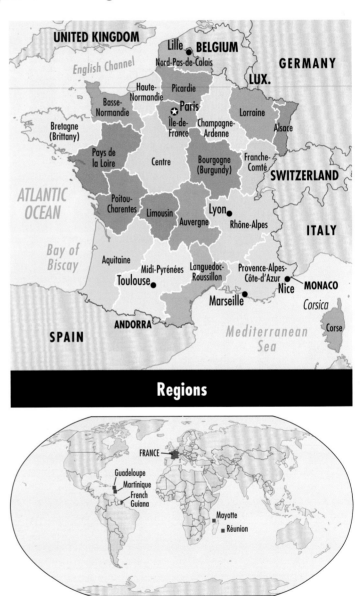

Regions

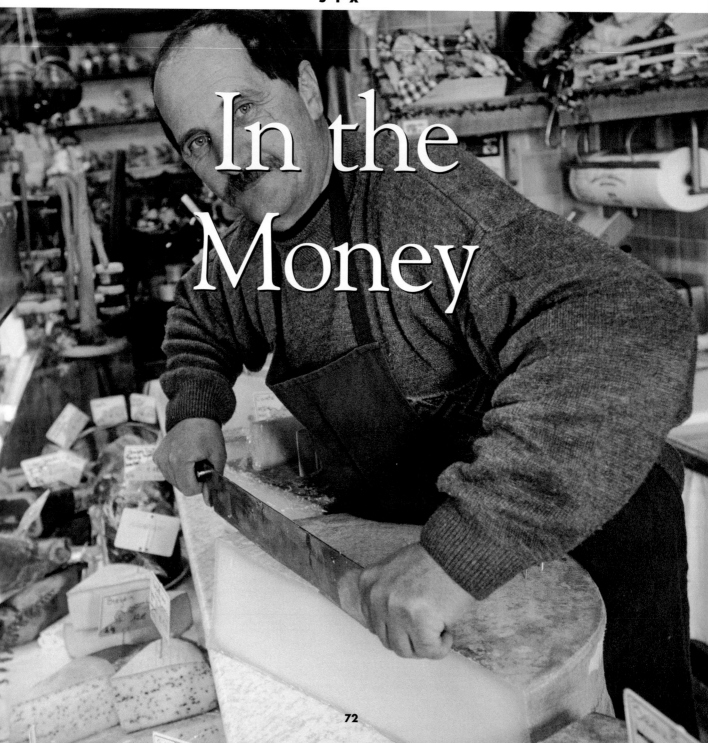

CHAPTER

SIX

In the Money

THE ECONOMY OF FRANCE HAS LONG MADE GOOD use of the country's natural and human resources. The country's pleasant climate and abundant farmland make it Europe's leading agricultural nation. Its well-trained and highly educated workforce allows France to dominate many industries, from aerospace to medicines. And its rich history, vibrant cities, and delightful landscape attract millions of tourists each year. As a result, France has the fifth-largest economy in the world, behind only the United States, Japan, Germany, and China.

Opposite: **France is known for producing many delicious food products, including cheese.**

From the Land

Although only about 4 percent of the French population works in agriculture, France is home to more than seven hundred thousand farms. Many grow grains, such as wheat, corn, and barley, helping to make the country the world's fifth-largest grain producer. Other important crops include sugar beets, peaches, beans, tomatoes, apples, and carrots.

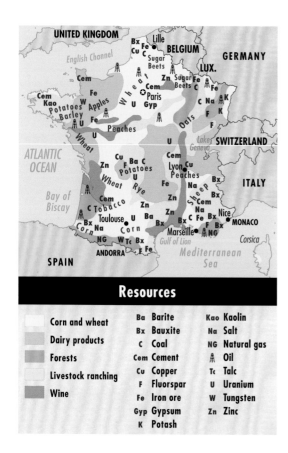

Resources

☐ Corn and wheat	Ba	Barite	Kao Kaolin
☐ Dairy products	Bx	Bauxite	Na Salt
☐ Forests	C	Coal	NG Natural gas
☐ Livestock ranching	Cem	Cement	⚒ Oil
☐ Wine	Cu	Copper	Tc Talc
	F	Fluorspar	U Uranium
	Fe	Iron ore	W Tungsten
	Gyp	Gypsum	Zn Zinc
	K	Potash	

A worker stacks baskets of grapes that will be turned into wine.

Lush vineyards, especially in the south of the country, produce grapes for France's wine industry. The country is famed for fine wines. Some varieties—such as burgundy, bordeaux, and champagne—are named after areas in France. Today, France is second only to Italy as the world's largest wine producer.

France's farms are also ideal for raising livestock, such as pigs, sheep, and goats. Farmers keep herds of cows for their milk, much of which is used to make cheese. France produces about four hundred different types of cheese.

Forestry is another important industry in France. In recent decades, the government has worked to increase the size of its forests,

What France Grows, Makes, and Mines

Agriculture (2009)

Wheat	38,332,200 metric tons
Sugar beets	35,066,600 metric tons
Cow's milk	23,341,000 metric tons

Manufacturing (2006, value added by manufacturing)

Chemical products	US$35,549,000,000
Transportation equipment	US$33,822,000,000
Fabricated metal products	US$27,754,000,000

Mining (2008)

Gypsum	3,500,000 metric tons
Talc	420,000 metric tons
Kaolin	300,000 metric tons

which now cover about one-third of France. These forests provide timber for construction and pulp for the paper industry. They also enhance the beauty of the French countryside, enticing millions of vacationers every year.

Manufacturing and Services

Manufacturing is another key component of France's economy. French industry, which employs about 24 percent of the nation's workers, makes a wide array of goods, including chemicals, processed foods, textiles, electronics, machinery, and medicines.

About 2.3 million vehicles were built in France in 2011.

France has a thriving automobile industry and is the world's fourth-largest exporter of cars. Its leading car companies include PSA Peugeot Citroën and Renault. France's Michelin is the largest tire company in the world. The city of Toulouse is the center of Europe's aviation industry. It produces aircraft for export to countries near and far, including the Airbus A380, the world's largest passenger plane.

France is also known for producing luxury goods. For many decades, French design houses such as Givenchy and Yves Saint Laurent have dominated haute couture (French for "high fashion"), the industry that creates extremely expensive clothing. Other luxurious French brands include Hermès, known for scarves and leather handbags; Lalique, for glassware; and Cartier, for fine jewelry and watches. International giants L'Oréal, Lancôme, and Estée Lauder lead France's large cosmetic industry, while brands such as Chanel and Guerlain help make France the biggest exporter of perfumes. The small town of Grasse on the Mediterranean Sea is home to dozens of perfume producers, and is sometimes called the perfume capital of the world.

The largest part of the French economy by far is the service industry. About 72 percent of French workers provide services to individuals or companies. Some work in retail stores. Others are involved in buying and selling real estate. Still others provide financial services. Banking and insurance are among the largest service industries in France.

France is the world's leader in producing perfume.

France has an unusually large number of workers who provide services to tourists. It is the most visited nation on the globe, welcoming more than seventy-five million tourists each year. About one million French people work in the thousands of hotels, hostels, restaurants, and attractions that cater to foreign guests.

Transportation and Energy

All sectors of France's economy are boosted by the country's excellent transportation system. Nearly every corner of France is accessible by its vast network of roadways. Even

High-speed trains travel from Paris to major cities throughout France.

more impressive is France's rail system. With about 20,000 miles (32,000 km) of track, train service connects all major cities and provides access to nearby countries. In the late twentieth century, France embarked on an ambitious program to develop high-speed trains, which can travel up to 200 miles per hour (320 kilometers per hour).

France has about 475 airports, including two of Europe's busiest, Orly and Charles de Gaulle (also called Roissy), both near Paris. The nation also boasts several excellent ports, including Calais and Le Havre on the English Channel and Marseille on the Mediterranean. Major rivers, such as the Seine, the Loire, and the Rhône, are used to transport goods throughout France. Tourists also enjoy Paris aboard sightseeing boats that travel up and down the Seine.

In addition to its excellent transportation system, the French economy benefits from the government's commitment to energy independence. France has only small oil reserves,

Barges transporting goods travel up and down major French rivers such as the Rhône.

Money Facts

The official currency of France is the euro (€), which is used by seventeen of the twenty-seven nations in the European Union. One euro is divided into one hundred cents. In 2012, €1 equaled US$1.23, and US$1.00 equaled about €0.81.

Bills come in values of 5, 10, 20, 50, 100, 200, and 500 euros. Each denomination is a different color. On the front is an image of a window or doorway, representing the spirit of openness among EU members. On the back is an illustration of a bridge, symbolizing the ties between the EU and the other nations of the world. The structures pictured on each bill represent a specific style of European architecture. For instance, the €20 note is blue and depicts cathedral windows and a bridge in the Gothic style.

Coins come in values of 1 and 2 euros, and 1, 2, 5, 10, 20, and 50 cents. A map of Europe appears on one side of euro coins. The other side varies, depending on which country issued the coins. In France, €1 and €2 coins depict a tree, symbolizing life and growth. Coins worth 1, 2, and 5 cents show a portrait of Marianne, a female figure who is a symbol of the French Republic. Coins worth 10, 20, and 50 cents depict La Semeuse, a beautiful woman sowing seeds, representing peace and prosperity.

so the French have to import most oil and gasoline that they use. In the 1970s, when the price of oil rose dramatically, the government encouraged its citizens to practice energy conservation. As a result of this program, France consumes about half as much oil per person as the United States does. The French government also invested in nuclear reactors, which supply most of the country's electricity. In recent years, though, some people have opposed France's nuclear energy program because of concerns about the possibility of a nuclear accident.

The French government pursues a variety of policies to help the average French worker. For instance, it requires employers to limit the workweek to thirty-five hours and to provide at least five weeks of paid vacation each year. Many programs help workers with small children by providing funds for child care and preschool and offering up to twenty-six weeks of paid parental leave after the birth of a child. In part because of these family-friendly policies, France has one of the highest rates of women in its workforce. About 47 percent of all French workers are women.

In recent years, however, the government has tried to reduce some of its generous benefits for workers in order to save money. For example, in 2010 conservative president Nicolas Sarkozy proposed raising the eligibility age for government-funded pensions, which provide money to workers after they retire. Millions of French people took to the streets to protest the change. Another challenge facing the French labor force is high unemployment, especially for young people and recent immigrants. If young people do find jobs, they are often in the low-paying service sector.

Another problem for the French economy is a financial crisis in the European Union. An economic downturn beginning in 2008 led some EU nations, such as Greece and Spain, into serious financial crisis. The European Union had to spend billions in bailouts to help these countries. Although France has a stronger economy than many other member nations, it has still been rocked by the financial instability of Europe and the new economic burdens on the European Union.

The French People

FRANCE IS HOME TO ABOUT SIXTY-SIX MILLION PEOPLE, making it the twenty-first most populated nation in the world. Of European nations, its population is the third largest, trailing only that of Russia and Germany. An additional two million French citizens live outside metropolitan France. Most are residents of France's far-flung overseas departments and other territories.

By world standards, the French are very healthy. Life expectancy for French men is about seventy-eight, while for French women it is eighty-four. Only about 25 percent of the French are younger than twenty.

The population's distribution throughout the country has changed dramatically since World War II. After the war, improvements in agriculture meant that fewer people were needed to work on farms. Many rural workers moved to cities to find jobs, and urban areas grew much bigger. Paris and the surrounding area doubled in population. Today, more than three out of every four people in France live in or near a city.

Opposite: **About one-quarter of French people live in rural areas.**

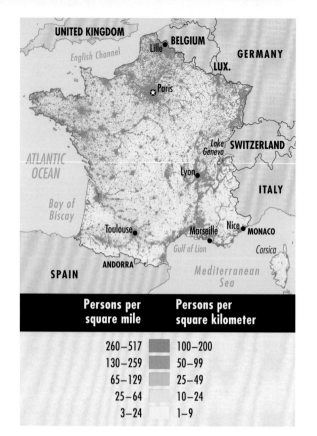

Persons per square mile	Persons per square kilometer
260–517	100–200
130–259	50–99
65–129	25–49
25–64	10–24
3–24	1–9

Population of Largest Cities (2011 est.)

Paris	2,300,000
Marseille	872,000
Lyon	472,000
Toulouse	435,000
Bordeaux	237,000
Lille	228,000

Ethnic Groups

Early in France's history, several waves of invaders entered the area and made it their home. The majority of the French people today can trace their ancestry back to these groups. Most French have some combination of Celtic, Roman, and Frankish heritage.

Families that have long lived near France's international boundaries are often ethnically linked to foreign neighbors. For instance, many people in the Alsace region that borders Germany are of Germanic ancestry, while French residents of the island of Corsica often have Italian roots.

Some of these groups share a culture that distinguishes them from other French people. For example, the Bretons, concentrated in the region of Brittany (Bretagne in French), are descended from Celtic peoples who immigrated to France from Great Britain more than one thousand years ago. In addition to sharing the Breton language, the Bretons today often gather to enjoy traditional music, dancing, and foods during the traditional festival of Fest Noz.

In southwestern France, the French Catalonians similarly embrace many of their ancestors' ways. Related to the much larger Catalonian population of northern Spain, they are known for their rich literary traditions, which date back to the Middle Ages.

A small number of Basque people also live in France near the Spanish border. They share the culture and language of the Basques of Spain. But while some Spanish Basques are seeking political independence, the Basques in France generally consider themselves French and feel comfortable in the larger French society.

Immigration to France

France has a long tradition of welcoming immigrants. Until the mid-twentieth century, most of them came from other European countries. In the years since, many immigrants

French Basques dance at a traditional wedding.

Ethnic Groups

French	87%
North African	9%
African and Caribbean	3%
Asian	1%

About a quarter of a million people in France are of Vietnamese descent.

arrived from former French colonies in North Africa, such as Algeria and Tunisia, and also from former French colonies in Asia, such as Vietnam. By law, the French government cannot compile exact statistics about the ethnic and racial characteristics of France's population, because of the belief that all French citizens, no matter their background, should merely be considered French. However, according to the French National Institute of Statistics, an estimated 19 percent of the French population is either foreign-born immigrants or their direct descendants.

At the height of postwar immigration between 1955 and 1975, many new arrivals settled in public housing projects near factories on the outskirts of large French cities. They continued to speak their native languages and observe the customs of their birth countries. They were often separated from mainstream French society by their skin color, religion, and French racial prejudices left over from the colonial period. Since the 1970s, periods of economic downturn have sparked resentment among white French against the immigrants and their children and grandchildren. French voters have shown increasing support for the National Front, a political party that strongly opposes immigration and has often been accused of following a racist agenda. In the first round of the May 2012 presidential election, party leader Marine Le Pen won nearly 18 percent of the vote. Her strong showing alarmed many French political figures, because they fear the National Front's agenda will only worsen the growing tensions in French society.

Marine Le Pen leads the National Front party, which opposes immigration.

Police arrested nearly three thousand people during riots in 2005.

These tensions have sometimes erupted into violence. Particularly devastating were a series of riots that broke out in Paris and other cities in late 2005. The rioters were mostly young people from poor ethnic neighborhoods. They were angry about the unacknowledged discrimination they had experienced in French society, a lack of opportunity to succeed, and the high unemployment rate among young people. The riots resulted in almost three thousand arrests and damage to about nine thousand cars, many of which rioters set ablaze.

A Shared Language

Despite their differences, the French people are almost all united by their language. Nearly everyone in France speaks and understands French. Many people in France also know a second language. Immigrants, for instance, also speak their native language, and businesspeople often know English or another European language.

France's history has helped shape the French language. It includes words that come from Celtic and German because of the invasions of Celtic and Frankish peoples. The French vocabulary also borrows words from other modern European languages, including Spanish, Italian, and English.

Because France's empire once controlled areas around the world, French has long been spoken in areas outside of France. Until recently, it was so common for highly educated people to learn French that it was the language of diplomats, officials who represent their countries in negotiations with foreign governments. Today, French remains the second most-studied language in the world, trailing only English. It is an official language of the United Nations and the Olympics, as well as twenty-nine countries around the world.

More than eighty daily newspapers are published in France.

Origins of the French Language

French is called a Romance language because it is derived from Latin, the language of ancient Rome. Latin was introduced into what is now France when the Roman army conquered the region in 51 BCE. About one thousand years ago, people in Paris began speaking a new dialect, or version of the language, which was distinct from Latin. In time, that dialect developed into the modern French language.

Regional Languages

Many French people are proud of their language as an expression of their country's rich literary, artistic, and philosophical traditions. In general, the French feel strongly that their language should be spoken and written correctly. Since its founding in 1882, the French public school system has stressed the importance of proper French spelling, grammar, and pronunciation to generations of students. The significance placed on the French language has its roots in the French Revolution. To promote the idea of equality and unity,

French schools teach in French and regional languages.

Common French Words and Phrases

Oui	Yes
Non	No
Bonjour	Hello/Good morning
Bonsoir	Hello/Good evening
Au revoir	Good-bye
Bonne nuit	Good night
Comment allez-vous?	How are you?
Bien	I'm fine.
Excusez-moi	Excuse me
S'il vous plaît	Please
Merci	Thank you

the government wanted all citizens to speak standard French, no matter their ethnicity, economic class, or social standing.

Until the 1970s, schools not only promoted proper French, but they also suppressed other languages that were spoken only in certain regions. Regional languages in France include Breton, Catalan, Corsican, Flemish, Basque, and German. Today, however, these local tongues are taught as part of France's diverse cultural heritage. In Corsica, for instance, some schools use French in half the classes, and Corsican in the other half.

The most widely spoken regional language in France is Occitan, which is still used in some rural areas of southern France. Like French, Occitan is derived from Latin, but it is more closely related to Spanish and Italian than to French. In the Middle Ages, an early form of Occitan was used by troubadours, traveling singers whose songs influenced European poetry. Native speakers of Occitan are becoming rarer, sparking efforts to preserve the language so it does not die out entirely.

Religious Life

ROMAN CATHOLICISM HAS TRADITIONALLY BEEN the dominant religion in France. Approximately 1,500 years ago, the French first began to adopt Catholicism, which became the official religion of the French kingdom. Because of its strong ties to Catholicism, France was often called the "eldest daughter" of the Catholic Church.

At the beginning of the twentieth century, the French government formally separated church and state. The government favors no religion over any other. Strongly committed to religious tolerance, the government maintains that all French citizens are free to hold any religious beliefs without restriction. Even though the French people are still largely Catholic, the Catholic Church receives no funds from the government. Some private schools that are run by the church, however, do receive a portion of their operating costs from the state.

Opposite: **Priests take part in a ceremony at the Notre-Dame Cathedral in Paris.**

A Catholic Nation

The government of France does not record statistics about the religious beliefs of its people. Although their exact numbers are not known, according to most estimates, about four out of every five people in France are Roman Catholics.

In some rural and more traditional areas, such as Brittany and Alsace, regular churchgoing continues to be an important part of life. But most of France has seen a dramatic drop in church attendance in recent decades, particularly among young people. Many French people who identify themselves as Catholic rarely go to church, except perhaps on a major religious holiday such as Christmas or Easter. Some nonpracticing Catholics still like to mark special occasions in their lives, such as marriages and baptisms, within their family's church. They also hold funerals there.

It is estimated that only 15 percent of French people regularly attend church services.

Lending a Hand

The French priest Abbé Pierre was the son of a wealthy industrialist who became a leading advocate for the homeless and the poor. Born Henri Antoine Grouès in 1912, he gave up his share of the family fortune and became a Catholic priest in 1938. During World War II, Grouès served in the French army and was a member of the French Resistance. At this time, he adopted the name "Abbé Pierre" (Abbot Pierre) to hide his identity.

Following the war, Abbé Pierre began speaking out in defense of the homeless. In 1954, he made a radio address urging the French to donate blankets, food, and money to help the thousands of homeless people suffering during a harsh winter. His moving speech received an overwhelming response. Abbé Pierre also started the Emmaus Movement, which helped create communities for the poor in dozens of countries.

After Abbé Pierre died in 2007, French president Jacques Chirac announced a national day of mourning in his memory. Still revered as a hero in France, in a televised poll Abbé Pierre was voted the third greatest Frenchman who ever lived, ranking behind only former French president Charles de Gaulle and scientist Louis Pasteur.

Catholic Traditions

Catholic holidays are celebrated by people throughout France. Despite the government's commitment to staying neutral in matters of religion, several of these Catholic holidays are also national holidays. These include Christmas, Easter Monday, and All Saints' Day. All workers, no matter their religious beliefs, get these days off.

Some French towns celebrate Pentecost with lively parades.

During the Christmas season, French families decorate their homes with Christmas trees and crèches—sets of tiny figurines arranged to create the scene of Jesus's birth. On Christmas Eve, many people attend a midnight mass (a Catholic church service) and return home for a special meal called the *réveillon*. The dishes served at this meal vary by region. In Alsace, the meal traditionally includes goose; in Burgundy (Bourgogne in French), turkey; and in Paris, foie gras (duck or goose liver) and oysters.

Another important Christian holiday in France is All Saints' Day, when the French take time to visit the burial sites of departed friends and family and decorate them with colorful flowers. Pentecost is celebrated with festivals. The town of Apt in Provence has put on a lively carnival and parade at Pentecost every year since the 1850s.

Another elaborate local holiday is Lyon's Festival of Lights, which begins on December 8, the date of the Feast of the Immaculate Conception. The festival has its origins in the seventeenth century. Fearing a plague, the citizens of Lyon prayed to Jesus's mother, Mary, who is said to have cleansed the city of disease. During the Festival of Lights, families illuminate their homes with candles in colored jars, while buildings, churches, and open spaces are set aglow with thousands of artificial lights.

France's Catholic heritage is also seen in its architecture. The country is filled with beautiful churches and cathedrals. Among the most spectacular are those in the Gothic architectural style, now considered one of the country's greatest artistic achievements. Meant to glorify God, the Gothic style features high arches and large areas of glass that fill these structures with light and give them a dramatic and grand presence. Some of the most spectacular Gothic cathedrals, such as Notre-Dame in Paris and Chartres Cathedral in the city of Chartres, are among the most visited attractions in France.

Catholic Holidays in France

Epiphany	January 6
Candlemas	February 2
Good Friday	March or April
Easter Sunday	March or April
Ascension Day	May or June
Pentecost	May or June
Midsummer's Day	June 24
Assumption Day	August 15
All Saints' Day	November 1
Feast of the Immaculate Conception	December 8
Christmas	December 25

Although France has a large Christian population, only about seven hundred thousand people there are Protestant. They belong to a variety of denominations, including Presbyterian and Lutheran. The most significant Protestant site in France is Taizé in the Burgundy region. There, Roger Schutz, a Swiss

Tourists line up to get into Notre-Dame Cathedral.

About half a million Jews live in France.

Protestant clergyman better known as Frère Roger (Brother Roger), established a monastery in 1940. Today, many thousands of young Christians of all faiths travel to Taizé to visit with one another and pray.

Jews are another significant religious minority in France. France has the largest Jewish population of any European country. About half the population of French Jews now lives in Paris.

Religion in France

Roman Catholic	81.4%
Muslim	6.9%
Protestant	1.6%
Jewish	0.9%
Buddhist	0.7%
Orthodox	0.3%
Other	8.1%

Jews have had a difficult history in France. During World War II, the Nazis and the Vichy regime deported more than seventy-five thousand Jews from France to death camps in eastern Europe. French Jews have also long been the targets of persecution and discrimination. In recent years, several synagogues, Jewish houses of worship, have been vandalized.

The second most common religion in France is Islam. France's Muslim population is the largest in western Europe, probably numbering about five million. Many Muslims live in Marseille and the surrounding area, and Paris and Lyon also have sizable Muslim populations.

Islam is a fairly new religion in France. It became common in the mid-twentieth century, when mass immigration from France's African colonies began. The Muslim population in France has continued to grow, but integration into French society has been difficult. Many French Muslims have faced racism, especially when they have asserted their own ethnic identities. In facing this challenge of being a diverse nation, France can look for inspiration in its long history of religious tolerance and time-tested commitment to the equality of all its people.

Religious Symbols in French Schools

In 2004, France's parliament passed a law that has stirred up controversy ever since. The law forbids students from wearing any obvious religious symbols in public schools. These include large Christian crosses, Jewish skullcaps, and Muslim headscarves. Legislators claimed the law was needed to preserve France's absolute separation of church and state.

The ban came on the heels of many instances of Muslim girls being punished by school officials for wearing headscarves. Many Muslim women believe that headscarves are necessary for them to fulfill their religious duty to dress modestly. The ban has caused anger among French Muslims, who feel it infringes on their religious freedom.

A Rich
Culture

THE FRENCH HAVE ACCOMPLISHED MUCH IN their history, and they are proud of their culture and achievements. In just about every art form—from painting to literature, from film to fashion—the French have made enormous contributions to world culture, inspiring artists everywhere.

Opposite: **Boy with a Small Whip,** by Pierre-Auguste Renoir. Renoir was a leader in the development of impressionism, an art style that emphasizes movement and light.

Art and Architecture

For many visitors to France, their trip would not be complete without spending time in one of the country's many excellent art museums. In Paris alone, dozens of museums showcase the work of France's most renowned artists. The Musée d'Orsay gathers paintings by Edgar Degas, Pierre-Auguste Renoir, Georges Seurat, and other modern masters of the late nineteenth century, while the Musée Rodin is devoted soley to the work of Auguste Rodin, considered one of the greatest sculptors of all time. But the most spectacular art museum in Paris is the Louvre. Its massive collection includes such famous

The Louvre

One of the largest museums in the world, the Louvre houses an incredible collection of art that includes approximately eight hundred thousand works. The building itself is an artistic wonder. Located in Paris on the right bank of the Seine River, the main complex was a royal palace until being transformed into a public building during the French Revolution. In 1989, to celebrate the two-hundredth anniversary of the revolution, a spectacular glass pyramid, designed by American architect I. M. Pei, was added to the museum as an entrance.

In the Louvre's galleries are some of the greatest treasures of ancient times, including objects made by the ancient Egyptians, Greeks, and Romans. Among its most famous works is the Venus de Milo, a Greek sculpture of the goddess of love.

The Louvre also has an incredible collection of paintings, including many masterpieces by Italian, Spanish, Dutch, Flemish, and American artists. The most popular painting is the *Mona Lisa* (left), a portrait created by Italian artist Leonardo da Vinci in the early sixteenth century. But to the French, the jewels of the Louvre's painting collection are the works of revered French masters, including Antoine Watteau, Jacques-Louis David, Gustave Courbet, and Édouard Manet.

The Louvre welcomes more than eight million visitors a year. In addition to the permanent collection, they come for the many exhibitions, lectures, films, and concerts that the museum sponsors.

French masterworks as *Oath of the Horatii* (1784) by Jacques-Louis David and *Liberty Leading the People* (1830) by Eugène Delacroix.

Because of its rich artistic heritage, Paris has long been a magnet for artists and art students. Many of the best artists from other countries—including the Dutch painter Vincent van Gogh and the Spanish artist Pablo Picasso—created some of their finest works while living in France. Today, the prestigious École des Beaux-Arts (School of Fine Arts) still attracts international students eager to become immersed in the French art scene.

Edgar Degas is renowned for his paintings of ballet dancers, one of which is shown here.

The Arc de Triomphe honors the people who fought in the French Revolution and the Napoleonic wars.

France's extraordinary contributions to architecture are apparent throughout the country. Its churches and cathedrals represent the finest examples of the Romanesque and Gothic styles. Versailles and other royal palaces built for French kings are considered architectural marvels, as are many of the best-known monuments in Paris. The Arc de Triomphe shows the influence of Roman culture on France, and the Eiffel Tower is a triumph of modern engineering. Built in 1889, it is the tallest structure in Paris and the most visited monument in the world.

Music, Literature, and Film

France's musical heritage is equally impressive. Most French cities have their own symphony orchestra and opera houses. Paris's newest is the Bastille Opera, the home of the Paris

The Little Sparrow

Through her songs of pain and heartbreak, Edith Piaf became one of France's most beloved entertainers. Born Edith Giovanna Gassion in 1915 in a Paris slum, she endured a desperate childhood. By the time she was fifteen, Edith was on her own, earning her living by singing on Paris streets for coins tossed by passersby.

One of her performances impressed Louis Leplée, the owner of a popular nightclub. He took her under his wing. Because of her tiny frame, he dubbed her "La Môme Piaf," meaning "Little Sparrow." This was the origin of her stage name. During World War II, she became a regular performer in theaters and cafés in German-occupied Paris. Her reputation soon grew beyond France's borders. In 1946, she achieved international success with her recording of "La Vie en Rose" ("Life in Pink").

Piaf's fans adored her songs of love, particularly of romance gone wrong. They also followed every development in her tumultuous love life. In 1960, she had a hit with the song "Non, Je Ne Regrette Rien" ("No, I Have No Regrets"), which many people considered an unapologetic assessment of her stormy life. Piaf died in 1963, but her songs continue to delight music lovers the world over.

National Opera. Notable French composers include Claude Debussy, Maurice Ravel, and Georges Bizet.

Well-known for their love of language, the French have made an indelible stamp on world literature. France's great novelists include Victor Hugo, whose *Les Misérables* (The Miserable) inspired an acclaimed musical, and Marcel Proust, whose seven-volume masterpiece *À la recherche du temps perdu* (published in English as *In Search of Lost Time*) helped shape modern literature. A pioneering aviator during World War II, Antoine de Saint-Exupéry is especially beloved in France for his novella *Le Petit Prince* (also published as *The Little Prince*), which French readers of the newspaper *Le Monde* voted the best book of the twentieth century.

Victor Hugo wrote such classic novels as *Les Misérables* and *The Hunchback of Notre-Dame*.

In drama, seventeenth-century playwright Molière is still considered one of the greatest crafters of comedy. In the modern era, Jean Cocteau was renowned for his reexaminations of ancient myths; and Eugène Ionesco helped develop the Theater of the Absurd, which showed the emptiness and pointlessness of modern life. Throughout history, the works of French philosophers, such as René Descartes, Blaise Pascal, Albert Camus, and Jean-Paul Sartre have also inspired readers to examine their lives and their place in the world.

Since the birth of moving pictures, a technology invented in France in 1895 by the Lumière brothers, the French have had a thriving movie industry. The French people are frequent moviegoers, and many theaters show both French and foreign films. In fact, France is the third-biggest film market, trailing only the United States and India.

Louis (right) and Auguste (left) Lumière are considered the world's first filmmakers. They held their first film screening in 1895.

French filmmakers are well known for their innovation. They were especially influential in the 1960s, when François Truffaut, Jean-Luc Godard, and other pioneers of the French New Wave experimented with new storytelling techniques and sophisticated subject matter. France's prominence in world cinema helps make the annual Cannes Film Festival an international sensation. Each spring, excited moviemakers bring their latest films to the beautiful resort city of Cannes on the Mediterranean. There, when all the screenings are over, all the moviemakers wait to find out if their movie will win the Palme d'Or (Golden Palm), one of the most prestigious awards a film can receive.

France's passion for the arts is rivaled only by its love of sports and the great outdoors. Along the coastlines of France, people sail, windsurf, and jet-ski. In mountainous regions, the French enjoy mountain biking in the summer and skiing in the winter. In village squares and urban parks everywhere, amateur athletes gather to play soccer, rugby, badminton, and tennis. And throughout the countryside are sites where city dwellers can camp and picnic on weekends.

Like most Europeans, the French are fanatics for soccer, which most of the world calls football. Their national team is called Les Bleus (The Blues), a nod to the color of their shirts. In 1998, French fans were thrilled when Les Bleus won the World Cup, the leading international soccer tournament, which was held in Paris that year. In 2006, the team again made it to the World Cup finals, but they lost the game to their Italian rivals.

France has competed in every modern Olympics and has hosted the summer games twice (in 1900 and 1924) and the

Pétanque

Since the early 1900s, the French have enjoyed a lively outdoor game called *pétanque*, which is played with hollow metal balls called *boules*. Players roll the boules on the ground, trying to get them as close as they can to a small wooden ball called a *cochonnet*. This traditional sport requires no special court, and just about anyone can play. Everyone, from young children to senior citizens, can join in the fun.

Zinedine Zidane

The stellar soccer career of Zinedine Zidane earned him the adoration of millions of fans in his native France. Zidane was born on June 23, 1972, in a rundown housing project in Marseille. His parents, immigrants from the North African country of Algeria, struggled to provide for their family. Despite his slight build, Zidane began to distinguish himself on the soccer field in his early teens. He was selected for the French Youth National Team before winning a spot with the Bordeaux soccer club.

Zidane began playing for Juventus, a prestigious team in Italy, in 1996. At the same time, he held a spot on France's national team. In 1998, France hosted the World Cup, an international soccer tournament played every four years. Zidane scored two of the three goals

that brought France its first World Cup win. Zidane not only became a star to sports fans. He also emerged as a hero to France's minority populations, particularly those of African heritage.

Zidane signed a four-year contract with the Spanish team Real Madrid in 2001. He was paid 66 million euros, then a record for a professional soccer player. In 2006, Zidane announced that he would retire after that year's World Cup. France lost in the finals, but Zidane scored his team's only goal.

Zidane remains an enormously popular figure in France and other countries. In 2011, an online poll conducted by the Union of European Football Associations (UEFA) ranked Zidane as the greatest player in the history of its Champions League.

winter games three times (in 1924, 1968, and 1992). Over the years, French teams have had particularly strong showings in cycling, fencing, and skiing. One of France's greatest Olympic athletes, Jean-Claude Killy, won three gold medals in skiing at the 1968 winter Olympics held in the French city of Grenoble.

For French auto racing fans, the 24 Hours of Le Mans is the most exciting event of the year. The grueling race takes place over the course of a full day, testing both speed and endurance.

Crowds line the route of the Tour de France.

But by far the country's most famous sporting event is the Tour de France. This three-week bicycle race attracts the greatest riders in the world. Each day, they compete for the right to wear the *maillot jaune*— a yellow jersey that is awarded to the overall leader. The course, which stretches more than 2,000 miles (3,200 km), changes each year but always ends in the center of Paris. Spectators gather all along the route, cheering on their favorite riders, but the loudest shouts are reserved for the final day, as the victor speeds into the capital city.

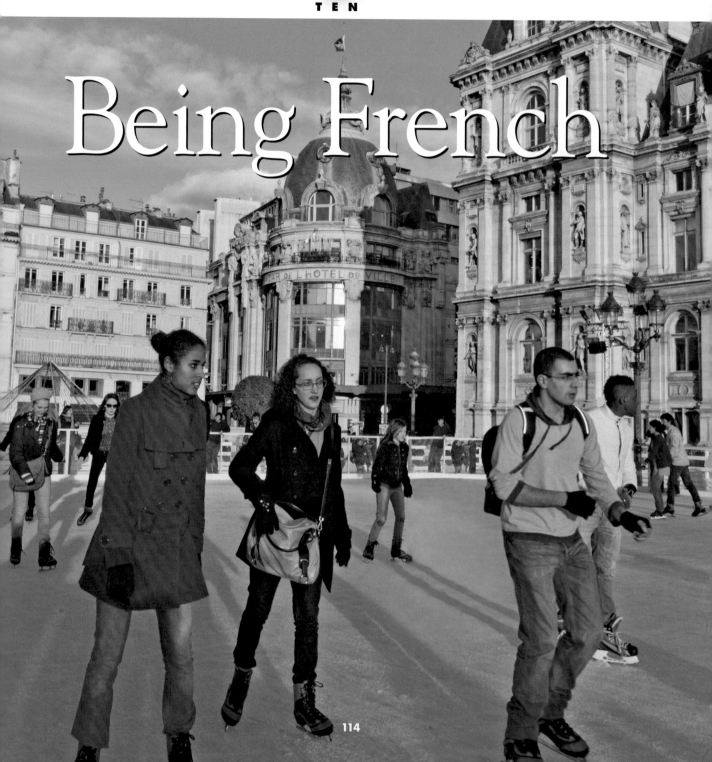

Being French

114

By world standards, the French people enjoy a very high quality of life. France offers excellent health care, and its educational system provides its citizens with excellent schools at little or no cost. Generous social services provided by the government assist the poor and elderly. Of all the wealthy nations, France has one of the smallest economic gaps between the rich and the poor.

But to the French, there are far more important things than being materially comfortable. They pride themselves on knowing how to live life to the fullest. In addition to being proud of their historical and artistic achievements, the French equally appreciate small, simple pleasures of daily life—from a delicious meal to an engaging conversation with friends and family.

Opposite: **Ice-skating is a popular winter activity in France.**

Growing Up

Traditionally, French households included several generations of a family—grandparents, parents, and children—all living together under the same roof. Today, such large households are less common, especially in urban areas. But family life remains important to the French. Even if they do not share a home, French adult children usually stay in close contact with their brothers, sisters, and parents. They often get together for a long, leisurely Sunday lunch or an outing to a sporting event or outdoor festival. Many families hold frequent reunions where family members can visit with relatives and renew their ties to one another.

Despite their closeness, French families retain a certain formality. Husbands and fathers are often authority figures who make the important decisions in their households. Parents make sure that their children are well behaved, both inside and outside the home. From a very young age, children are expected to have good manners. If children misbehave or lack self-control, they are told it reflects badly on their entire family.

French schools have an average of about twenty-three students in a class, the same as in the United States.

Formal schooling is also a serious matter for French children. Most begin their education at the age of three, when the majority of children attend free, government-run nursery schools. All children are required to go to school from the ages of six to sixteen, although most students continue on until at least age eighteen. During most of those years, French students are taught the same national curriculum. The lessons are often

A mother walks her children to school. On average, families in France have two children.

Coupe de Mariage

At many French weddings, the newlyweds receive a special gift called a *coupe de mariage*, or "marriage cup." This decorative two-handled cup, usually made of silver, is engraved with the couple's names and their wedding date. Later, the couple will add the names and birth dates of their children. During the reception, the bride and groom drink wine from the cup. Traditionally, a small piece of toast was added to the wine to ensure the newlyweds would have a happy and healthy life together. The toast in the coupe de mariage probably inspired the modern wedding toast—a ritual during which guests raise a glass to the couple to celebrate their union.

Playing Escargot

Escargot—French for "snail"—is a delicacy enjoyed by French diners. But to the children of France, escargot is also a traditional outdoor game. Similar to hopscotch, escargot is played on a "board" drawn with chalk on a sidewalk or driveway. The board is made up of about fifteen, or sometimes more, numbered squares arranged in a spiral, mimicking the shape of a snail's shell. The middle space is the resting spot.

Each player takes turns, hopping on one foot on each square to move into the spiral and then out of it. If players step on a line on any square, they lose their turn. If they make it all the way in and out of the "shell," they get to put their initials on the square of their choosing. Players can rest on any square they have initialed themselves, but they have to jump over a square with someone else's initials. The game continues until none of the players can hop to the center resting spot. The player with the most initialed squares is the winner.

challenging, with even young children studying subjects such as philosophy and high-level mathematics. In high school, called *lycée*, students can take either an academic or a vocational course of study. Earning an academic degree, or *baccalaréat*, qualifies students for a spot at a public university, where tuition is almost free. The best students apply to the highly competitive *grandes écoles* (great schools). If they graduate from one of these universities, they are virtually guaranteed a well-paid career in industry, government, or politics.

Although the French workforce is highly productive, people in France work fewer hours than people in nearly any other country. French law limits the workweek to thirty-five hours and requires that employees get five weeks of paid vacation each year, although some workers receive more.

The French make the most of this time off. In late July and August, when the weather is warm and sunny, it sometimes seems as though everyone is on vacation. Many people flock to the beaches and resorts in the south. Others relax and spend time with their families in the countryside. In urban areas, espe-

A long, relaxed lunch is a tradition in France.

Walking is one of the best ways to get around Paris.

cially Paris, housing costs are high, and most people can only afford small apartments. But they often have enough left over to rent or buy larger vacation homes in rural areas. France has more people with second homes than any other country.

While Parisians and other city dwellers enjoy brief escapes to the countryside, they also have a wealth of leisure options close to home. Among the most walkable cities in the world, Paris is filled with shops, boutiques, and nightclubs. People take advantage of how easily they can get to all these places, whether on foot, on bike, or by a subway ride. Simply strolling around the city and taking in its beautiful architecture, parks, and gardens can be entertaining at all times of the day and night.

A Gourmet Nation

Throughout France, one form of entertainment is greatly favored—eating a wonderful meal. French cooking is an art, and many of the greatest chefs have been trained in Paris.

French cooking is known for its rich sauces, often made with cream or wine, but every region of France has its own signature dish. Marseille is famous for bouillabaisse, a spicy fish stew. Burgundy is renowned for escargot, cooked snails often flavored with butter, garlic, and herbs. The cuisine of Alsace features sausage like that of Germany, its neighbor to the east. Dishes from Provence show a Mediterranean influence, featuring olive oil, tomatoes, garlic, and peppers.

Traditional French cuisine features rich sauces.

Quiche Lorraine

Since the sixteenth century, the French living in the region of Lorraine have enjoyed a tasty baked egg-and-bacon pie they call quiche. Today, quiche Lorraine is a favorite dish throughout France. Although traditional French chefs usually do not add cheese to quiche Lorraine, this more modern version includes a generous helping of Gruyère, a cheese similar to Swiss. Have an adult help you with this recipe.

Ingredients

4 slices of cooked bacon

1 9-inch premade piecrust

1 cup of shredded Gruyère cheese

4 eggs

1 cup of half-and-half or heavy cream

¼ teaspoon salt

⅛ teaspoon pepper

⅛ teaspoon nutmeg

Directions

Preheat the oven to 375°F. Crumble the bacon and spread it on the bottom of the piecrust. Top the bacon with cheese. Next, beat the eggs in a large bowl with the cream, salt, pepper, and nutmeg. Pour the egg mixture into the piecrust. Bake the quiche for about 40 to 45 minutes until the eggs are fully cooked. Allow it to cool slightly, and then cut it into wedges. Quiche Lorraine is often served with a small side salad. Enjoy!

French cities, especially Paris and Lyon, are known for their many excellent restaurants. Meals at high-end restaurants can last for hours and often feature many different courses, each with a different wine. More casual restaurants, called bistros, offer quick, simple, but delicious meals at a low price.

For a light meal, a cup of coffee, or a glass of wine, the French (often with their pet dogs in tow) duck into one of the cafés that line city streets. Throughout the day, cafés are full of people passing time, leisurely reading a newspaper, watching soccer on television, or merely watching the parade of pass-ersby on the sidewalk. Often friends will meet at a café and

Parisians flock to outdoor cafés, where they can sit and talk for hours.

talk for hours. The French are known for their love of conversation. In these informal debates on anything from politics to movies, everyone tries to win the argument or at least come up with the cleverest remark.

Enjoying the Good Life

France's finest restaurants serve elaborate, sumptuous dishes, but the everyday fare people fix for themselves is usually quite simple. Breakfast might be a pastry or croissant with a café au

Buttery, flaky pastries called croissants are a common French breakfast.

lait (coffee with milk). Traditionally, lunch was the main meal of the day and often lasted several hours. Today, in cities especially, lunch is more often a quick meal made up of perhaps an omelet and a salad or steak frites (steak with French fries). Dinner might feature ham, roast chicken, or fresh seafood. The French often eat bread and sip wine throughout their meals, although mineral water and juice are also common beverages. Everyday desserts include fresh fruit or a selection of cheeses.

The French buy much of their food in supermarkets, but they also frequent outdoor markets. Every town has one or two market days a week, where local farmers sell fresh meat, cheese, fruits, and vegetables in the town square. In Paris and other cities, outdoor markets also sell other goods, such as secondhand clothing and antique furniture. Wandering through

Many French people buy fruits and vegetables at outdoor markets.

A military parade marches through the center of Paris on Bastille Day.

the stalls looking for a bargain is a cherished weekend entertainment, often shared with family and friends.

Other favorite activities include attending festivals. In February, Nice hosts Carnaval, which features floats, fireworks, and masked balls. In June, Bordeaux celebrates the latest grape harvest with a wine festival. In July, Avignon holds a month-long celebration of theater and the arts. In the summer, Parisians who cannot get to the coast for vacation enjoy the Paris-Plages (Paris beaches). The city blocks off roads along the Seine and fills them with sand, palm trees, umbrellas, and beach chairs, where people can lounge and get some sun. In September, Parisians mark the end of the vacation season with *la rentrée* (the return), a collection of cultural events held throughout the city.

Everywhere in France, July 14 is a day of great celebration. Called National Day or Bastille Day, it commemorates the storming of the Bastille prison in 1789, an event that helped spark the French Revolution. This national holiday's festivities include parades and fireworks displays.

No matter their backgrounds, all the French come together on Bastille Day to cheer their common heritage and culture. But in France, pride in being French is hardly a one-day affair. It is something the French people always feel, whether they are reflecting on their nation's past glories or looking with anticipation to what the future might bring.

Public Holidays

New Year's Day	January 1
Monday after Easter	March or April
Labor Day	May 1
Victory in Europe Day	May 8
Ascension Day	May
Monday after Pentecost	May or June
National Day	July 14
Assumption Day	August 15
All Saints' Day	November 1
Armistice Day	November 11
Christmas	December 25

Timeline

French History

Prehistoric people paint the walls of the Lascaux caves.	ca. 18,000 BCE
Celtic tribes occupy what is now France.	ca. 450 BCE
Roman general Julius Caesar conquers France, which was then called Gaul.	51 BCE
The Frankish king Clovis begins his rule.	481 CE
Charlemagne declares himself the emperor of the Holy Roman Empire, which includes France.	800
An epidemic of bubonic plague breaks out in France.	1348
France battles England in a series of conflicts known as the Hundred Years' War.	1337–1453
Joan of Arc leads French troops against an English force at Orléans.	1429
King Henry IV issues the Edict of Nantes, legalizing Protestantism in France.	1598
Louis XIV begins his seventy-two-year reign.	1643
French citizens storm the Bastille prison, marking the beginning of the French Revolution.	1789

World History

ca. 2500 BCE	The Egyptians build the pyramids and the Sphinx in Giza.
ca. 563 BCE	The Buddha is born in India.
313 CE	The Roman emperor Constantine legalizes Christianity.
610	The Prophet Muhammad begins preaching a new religion called Islam.
1054	The Eastern (Orthodox) and Western (Roman Catholic) Churches break apart.
1095	The Crusades begin.
1215	King John seals the Magna Carta.
1300s	The Renaissance begins in Italy.
1347	The plague sweeps through Europe.
1453	Ottoman Turks capture Constantinople, conquering the Byzantine Empire.
1492	Columbus arrives in North America.
1500s	Reformers break away from the Catholic Church, and Protestantism is born.

French History

King Louis XVI and Queen Marie Antoinette are beheaded.	1793
Napoléon Bonaparte names himself emperor of France.	1804
France fights Germany and its allies during World War I.	1914–1918
The German army invades France during World War II.	1940
Allied troops liberate Paris from German occupation.	1944
France adopts a new constitution.	1958
Charles de Gaulle becomes the president of France.	1959
Algeria becomes independent from France.	1962
Student and worker demonstrations force reforms in the French government.	1968
France joins the European Union.	1993
France and other European Union nations begin using the euro as their currency.	1999
France is rocked by a series of riots by impoverished young immigrants.	2005
François Hollande becomes president.	2012

World History

1776	The U.S. Declaration of Independence is signed.
1789	The French Revolution begins.
1865	The American Civil War ends.
1879	The first practical lightbulb is invented.
1914	World War I begins.
1917	The Bolshevik Revolution brings communism to Russia.
1929	A worldwide economic depression begins.
1939	World War II begins.
1945	World War II ends.
1969	Humans land on the Moon.
1975	The Vietnam War ends.
1989	The Berlin Wall is torn down as communism crumbles in Eastern Europe.
1991	The Soviet Union breaks into separate states.
2001	Terrorists attack the World Trade Center in New York City and the Pentagon near Washington, D.C.
2004	A tsunami in the Indian Ocean destroys coastlines in Africa, India, and Southeast Asia.
2008	The United States elects its first African American president.

Fast Facts

Official name: French Republic

Capital: Paris

Official language: French

Paris

FRANCE
- Cities of over 200,000 people
- Other cities
- National capital

0 150 miles
0 150 kilometers

NETHERLANDS

North Sea

UNITED KINGDOM

BELGIUM

LUXEMBOURG

GERMANY

Calais Dunkerque

Lille Valenciennes

English Channel

Dieppe

Cherbourg Le Havre Rouen Amiens Sedan

Giverny Reims Verdun Metz

Saint-Malo Bayeux Caen Paris Châlons-en-Champagne Nancy Strasbourg

Brest Vaucouleurs

Chartres Troyes Mulhouse AUSTRIA

Rennes Le Mans Orléans Auxerre

Lorient Carnac Angers Tours Dijon Besançon LIECHTENSTEIN

Saint-Nazaire Nantes Bourges SWITZERLAND

La Roche-sur-Yon Poitiers Moulins Taizé Lake Geneva

Niort Vichy

ATLANTIC OCEAN La Rochelle Limoges Clermont-Ferrand Lyon Chambéry

Tulle Saint-Étienne Vanoise Natl. Park ITALY

Bordeaux Lascaux caves Valence Grenoble Écrins Natl. Park Mercantour Natl. Park

Bay of Biscay Mende Cévennes Natl. Park Avignon Nice

Mont-de-Marsan Rodez Toulouse Nîmes Aix-en-Provence MONACO

Bayonne Pau Pyrénées Occidentales Natl. Park Montpellier Apt Cannes Bastia

Canal du Midi Marseille Toulon Calvi

SPAIN Perpignan Gulf of Lion Corsica Aléria

Cerbère Ajaccio

ANDORRA Mediterranean Sea Bonifacio

Rhine R. Seine R. Loire R. Saône R. Rhône R. Garonne R.

France

French flag

Mont Blanc

Official religion:	None
Year of founding:	1792
National anthem:	"La Marseillaise" ("Song of Marseille")
Type of government:	Republic
Head of state:	President
Head of government:	Prime minister
Area (metropolitan France):	212,935 square miles (551,500 sq km)
Latitude and longitude of geographic center (metropolitan France):	46° N, 2° E
Bordering countries:	Spain and Andorra to the southwest; Belgium and Luxembourg to the northeast; Germany, Switzerland, Italy, and Monaco to the east
Highest elevation:	Mont Blanc, 15,771 feet (4,807 m) above sea level
Lowest elevation:	Rhône River delta, 7 feet (2 m) below sea level
Highest average temperature:	75°F (24°C) in July in Paris
Lowest average temperature:	34°F (1°C) in January in Paris
Average annual rainfall:	26 inches (66 cm) in Paris

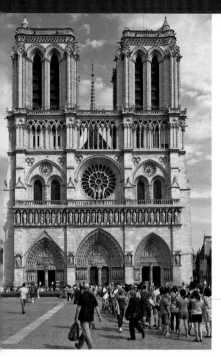

Notre-Dame Cathedral

National population (2011 est.): 65,821,885

Population of major cities (2011 est.):

Paris	2,300,000
Marseille	872,000
Lyon	472,000
Toulouse	435,000
Bordeaux	237,000
Lille	228,000

Landmarks:
- ▶ *Canal du Midi*, Toulouse
- ▶ *Eiffel Tower*, Paris
- ▶ *Lascaux caves*, Montignac
- ▶ *Louvre Museum*, Paris
- ▶ *Notre-Dame Cathedral*, Paris

Economy: France has the fifth-largest economy in the world. It leads Europe in agricultural production and manufactures a wide variety of goods, including textiles, electronics, automobiles, aircraft, chemicals, processed foods, and medicines. The service sector is dominated by France's thriving tourist industry, which caters to more than seventy-five million foreign visitors each year. Major agricultural products include wheat, sugar beets, peaches, tomatoes, apples, grapes, and milk.

Currency

Currency: The euro. In June 2012, €1 equaled US$1.23, and US$1.00 equaled about €0.81.

System of weights and measures: Metric system

Literacy rate (2006): 99%

Schoolchildren

Voltaire

Common French words and phrases:

Oui	Yes
Non	No
Bonjour	Hello/Good morning
Bonsoir	Hello/Good evening
Au revoir	Good-bye
Bonne nuit	Good night
Comment allez-vous?	How are you?
Bien	I'm fine.
Excusez-moi	Excuse me
S'il vous plaît	Please
Merci	Thank you

Prominent French people:

Napoléon Bonaparte (1769–1821)
General and emperor

Charles de Gaulle (1890–1970)
General and president

Joan of Arc (ca. 1412–1431)
Military leader and saint

Claude Monet (1840–1926)
Painter

Louis Pasteur (1822–1895)
Scientist

Edith Piaf (1915–1963)
Singer

Voltaire (1694–1778)
Writer and philosopher

Zinedine Zidane (1972–)
Soccer player

To Find Out More

Books

▶ Asselin, Gilles, and Ruth Mastron. *Au Contraire! Figuring Out the French*. Boston: Intercultural Press, 2010.

▶ Davenport, John C. *The French Revolution and the Rise of Napoleon*. New York: Chelsea House Publishers, 2011.

▶ Rossi, Renzo. *In the Sun King's Paris with Molière*. New York: Marshall Cavendish Benchmark, 2009.

▶ Wilkinson, Philip. *Joan of Arc: The Teenager Who Saved Her Nation*. Washington, DC: National Geographic Society, 2007.

Music

▶ Edith Piaf. *Eternelle*. London: EMI Classics: 2002.

▶ Rattle, Simon. *Debussy/Ravel: Orchestral Works*. London: EMI Classics: 2008.

▶ Visit this Scholastic Web site for more information on France:
www.factsfornow.scholastic.com
Enter the keyword France

Index

Page numbers in *italics* indicate illustrations.

Meet the Author

A GRADUATE OF SWARTHMORE COLLEGE, LIZ Sonneborn is a full-time writer living in Brooklyn, New York. She has written more than ninety nonfiction books for children, young adults, and adults on a wide variety of subjects. Her books include *The American West: An Illustrated History*, *A to Z of American Indian Women*, *The Ancient Kushites*, *The Vietnamese Americans*, *Chronology of American Indian History*, *Guglielmo Marconi*, and *The Environmental Movement*.

Sonneborn has written several books for the Enchantment of the World series, including *Canada*, *Pakistan*, and *Iraq*. She was thrilled to take on *France*, partly because when she was a young reader, she was obsessed with the country. "When I was seven," she explains, "I had a huge poster of the Eiffel Tower on my bedroom wall. I thought it was so beautiful and glamorous. I think I was in sixth grade when I chose to do a school project about famous French people. I wrote up biographical sketches of about two dozen public figures and drew pictures of each of them. I remember working especially hard on the portraits of French president Charles de Gaulle and film actress Brigitte Bardot. I got an A+."

With so much information available, finding research material on French history and culture was an easy task. But writing about the current economic slump, recent ethnic tensions, and the nation's changing political environment required studying the positions and biases of many magazine and newspaper articles. "Researching how France is responding to these shifts was the biggest challenge in writing this book," Sonneborn says.

Sonneborn has traveled to France several times, but in her Brooklyn neighborhood, a little bit of France is always nearby. "There is an enclave of French immigrants in my area, so when I walk down the streets, it's not at all unusual to pass people speaking in French," she says. "There is an annual celebration every July 14th centered on Brooklyn's Smith Street, which I've read is the largest Bastille Day celebration outside of France. It's always a fun day."

Meet the Consultant

Brett Bowles is an associate professor of French studies at Indiana University, Bloomington. A specialist in twentieth-century France, he focuses his research and teaching on cinema and cultural history. He is the author of many journal articles, as well as the book *Marcel Pagnol* (Manchester University Press, 2012) and a collection of essays on the politics of cinema in France and Germany. He is co-editor of the journal *Modern and Contemporary France* and serves on the editorial boards of *French Historical Studies*, *French History*, and the *Historical Journal of Film, Radio, and Television*.

Photo Credits